Wonders

Reading/Writing Companion

Mc
Graw
Hill

mheducation.com/prek-12

Send all inquiries to:
McGraw Hill
1325 Avenue of the Americas
New York, NY 10019

ISBN: 978-1-26-576729-7
MHID: 1-26-576729-7

Printed in the United States of America.

4 5 6 7 8 9 LMN 26 25 24 23 22   A

Welcome to
WONDERS!

We're here to help you set goals to build on the amazing things you already know. We'll also help you reflect on everything you'll learn.

Let's start by taking a look at the incredible things you'll do this year.

You'll build knowledge on exciting topics and find answers to interesting questions.

You'll read fascinating fiction, informational texts, and poetry and respond to what you read with your own thoughts and ideas.

And you'll research and write stories, poems, and essays of your own!

Here's a sneak peek at how you'll do it all.

"Let's go!"

You'll explore new ideas by reading groups of different texts about the same topic. These groups of texts are called *text sets*.

At the beginning of a text set, we'll help you set goals on the My Goals page. You'll see a bar with four boxes beneath each goal. Think about what you already know to fill in the bar. Here's an example.

I can read and understand narrative nonfiction.

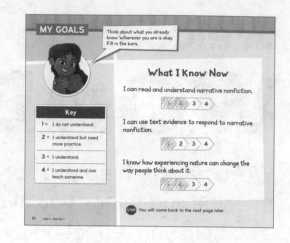

As you move through a text set, you'll explore an essential question and build your knowledge of a topic until you're ready to write about it yourself.

You'll also learn skills that will help you reach your text set goals. At the end of lessons, you'll see a new Check In bar with four boxes.

CHECK IN 1 2 3 4

Reflect on how well you understood a lesson to fill in the bar.

Here are some questions you can ask yourself.

- Was I able to complete the task?

- Was it easy, or was it hard?

- Do I think I need more practice?

You have plenty of tools and resources to learn more, such as anchor charts and center activities. You can also reread a lesson or ask a teacher or peer for help.

It's okay if I think I need more practice. The most important thing is that I do my best and keep learning!

Thinking about what works best for me will help me choose what to do next.

At the end of each text set, you'll show off the knowledge you built by completing a fun task. Then you'll return to the second My Goals page where we'll help you reflect on all that you learned.

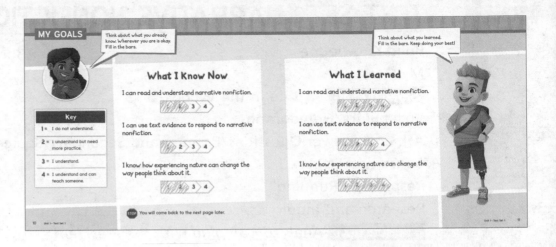

I'll fill in a new set of bars to show how far I've come. I started at 2, but now I'm at 4 because I can read and understand narrative nonfiction well enough to teach a friend.

I'll follow the same steps as I write my own stories, essays, and poems. I own my learning, and you can own yours!

"Let's get started!"

TEXT SET 1 **NARRATIVE NONFICTION**

TEXT SET 2 **REALISTIC FICTION**

TEXT SET 3 **ARGUMENTATIVE TEXT**

EXTENDED WRITING

CONNECT AND REFLECT

Digital Tools
Find this eBook and other resources at **my.mheducation.com**

Blend Images - JGI/Jamie Grill/Brand X Pictures/Getty Images

TEXT SET 1 **EXPOSITORY TEXT**

TEXT SET 2 **FOLKTALE**

TEXT SET 3 **POETRY**

EXTENDED WRITING

CONNECT AND REFLECT

Digital Tools

Find this eBook and other resources at **my.mheducation.com**

Build Knowledge

Essential Question

How can experiencing nature change the way you think about it?

Build Vocabulary

Write new words you learned about how experiencing nature can affect people. Draw lines and circles for the words you write.

We appreciate our natural world.

How Experiencing Nature Affects People

Go online to **my.mheducation.com** and read the "Protecting Our Parks" Blast. Think about your experiences with nature. Why are parks important to society? Then blast back your response.

Think about what you already know. Wherever you are is okay. Fill in the bars.

What I Know Now

I can read and understand narrative nonfiction.

| 1 | 2 | 3 | 4 |

I can use text evidence to respond to narrative nonfiction.

| 1 | 2 | 3 | 4 |

I know how experiencing nature can change the way people think about it.

| 1 | 2 | 3 | 4 |

Key
1 = I do not understand.
2 = I understand but need more practice.
3 = I understand.
4 = I understand and can teach someone.

 You will come back to the next page later.

Think about what you learned.
Fill in the bars. Keep doing your best!

What I Learned

I can read and understand narrative nonfiction.

1   2   3   4

I can use text evidence to respond to narrative nonfiction.

1   2   3   4

I know how experiencing nature can change the way people think about it.

1   2   3   4

My Goal I can read and understand narrative nonfiction.

TAKE NOTES

As you read, make note of interesting words and important details.

A Life in the Woods

Essential Question

How can experiencing nature change the way you think about it?

Read about how Thoreau's stay in the woods changed his view of nature.

Into the Woods

Henry David Thoreau raised his pen to write, but the chatter of guests in the next room filled his ears. He stared at the page. "Concord, 1841" was all that he had written. How would he write a book with such noise in his family's house? Thoreau headed outside, shutting the door with **emphasis**. He would have to find a place of his own.

Thoreau walked out of town. Tall white pines soon replaced the painted houses. He listened to the rustling of the leaves. What if I could stay here, he thought. He could live off the land, close to nature, and begin his book. It would take work, but he could do it.

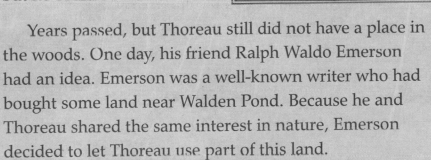

Years passed, but Thoreau still did not have a place in the woods. One day, his friend Ralph Waldo Emerson had an idea. Emerson was a well-known writer who had bought some land near Walden Pond. Because he and Thoreau shared the same interest in nature, Emerson decided to let Thoreau use part of this land.

In March of 1845, Thoreau began to build a cabin. By July, it was ready. He could live and write in the woods.

FIND TEXT EVIDENCE

Read

Paragraphs 1–2

Cause and Effect

What was the effect of Thoreau walking out of town? **Underline** the text evidence.

Homographs

The word *leaves* has more than one meaning. **Draw a box** around context clues that give the meaning.

Paragraphs 3–4

Ask and Answer Questions

What question can you ask and answer about Thoreau?

Reread

Author's Craft

How does the author help you visualize Thoreau's experience as he walks out of town?

FIND TEXT EVIDENCE

Read

Paragraph 1

Ask and Answer Questions

What is a question you can ask and answer about Thoreau?

_____

_____

_____

Paragraphs 2–3

Cause and Effect

Circle the signal word that helps you identify why Thoreau thinks the loon is laughing at him. Then **underline** what caused him to think this.

Primary Sources

Look at the text from Thoreau's journal. What impressed him?

_____

_____

_____

Reread

Author's Craft

Why might the author have included Thoreau's journal here?

Cabin Life

Thoreau's move to the woods **indicated** that he liked to be alone. But Thoreau did not feel that way. "I have a great deal of company in my house," he wrote. Red squirrels woke him by running up and down the **sheer** sides of his cabin. A snowshoe hare lived in the **debris** under his cabin, thumping against the floorboards. A sparrow once perched on his shoulder. Thoreau recorded these experiences in his journal. How easily writing came to him with the beauty of nature around him!

On Walden Pond

Thoreau was a **naturalist**. He noticed the habits of animals. Each **encounter** showed him something new. One afternoon, Thoreau tried to get a close look at a loon, but the bird quickly dove into the pond. He knew loons could travel long distances under water, so he guessed where it would come up. But every time Thoreau paddled to one spot, the loon came up somewhere else and let out a call—a howling laugh. What a silly loon, Thoreau thought. But after a while, Thoreau felt as though the bird was laughing at him because he still could not catch up to it. Thoreau wrote in his journal:

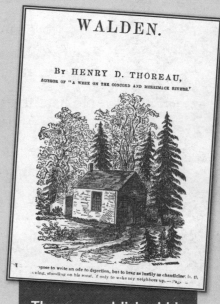

WALDEN.

By HENRY D. THOREAU,
AUTHOR OF "A WEEK ON THE CONCORD AND MERRIMACK RIVERS,"

Thoreau published his book *Walden* in 1854.

His white breast, the stillness of the air, and the smoothness of the water were all against him. At length he uttered one of those prolonged howls, as if calling on the god of the loons to aid him, and immediately there came a wind from the east and rippled the surface, and filled the whole air with misty rain, and I was impressed.

Loons are still a common sight on Walden Pond.

The **spectacular** scene made Thoreau wonder at the loon. It no longer seemed a silly animal, but one with some mysterious power. As months went by, Thoreau also became aware of each animal's ability to stay alive. "His power of observation seemed to indicate additional senses," Emerson once remarked. In winter, as he warmed his cabin by fire, he watched in awe as the moles warmed their nest by their own body heat. He understood forest life as never before.

Back to Concord

Like the geese that move to new ponds at the season's end, so too did Thoreau leave Walden. He had done what he had set out to do, and had learned much from the woods around him. He packed his few belongings and his stack of journals and returned to Concord. Now, he would turn his journal entries into a book. **Generations** to come would know life on Walden Pond!

Summarize

Use your notes to summarize important details of Thoreau's experience living by Walden Pond.

NARRATIVE NONFICTION

FIND TEXT EVIDENCE

Read

Paragraph 1

Cause and Effect

Write a sentence that explains what caused Thoreau to understand "forest life as never before."

_____

_____

_____

Paragraph 2

Ask and Answer Questions

What question can you ask to check your understanding of the second paragraph? Write your question.

_____

_____

Underline text evidence that helps you answer your question.

Reread

Author's Craft

How does the author show that Thoreau has changed by the end?

Vocabulary

Use the example sentences to talk with a partner about each word. Then answer the questions.

debris

The science class picked up **debris** that had washed up on the beach.

What is a synonym for *debris*?

_____

_____

emphasis

When Elena said, "Shhh," she put her finger to her lips for **emphasis**.

How can you show emphasis when you talk?

_____

_____

encounter

During a hike, you might have an **encounter** with a butterfly.

What is a synonym for *encounter*?

_____

_____

generations

My grandma has a pie recipe that has been in my family for many **generations**.

What is something students of your generation like to do?

_____

_____

indicated

The thermostat **indicated** that it was hot outside.

What is a synonym for *indicated*?

_____

_____

 Build Your Word List Pick a word you found interesting in the selection you read. Look up synonyms and antonyms of the word in a thesaurus and write them in your reader's notebook.

naturalist

The **naturalist** told us about many of the plants and animals she studied.

What is something you might ask a naturalist?

_____

_____

_____

sheer

When we looked up at the **sheer** rock wall, we knew it would be impossible to climb.

What else might you describe as sheer?

_____

_____

_____

spectacular

The mountaintop provides **spectacular** views.

What else might you describe as spectacular?

_____

Homographs

Homographs are words that are spelled the same but have different meanings and may be pronounced differently. Use sentence clues to help you choose the correct meaning and pronunciation of a homograph. A dictionary can also help you with finding the meaning and pronunciation of the word.

🔍 FIND TEXT EVIDENCE

When I read the fourth sentence of "On Walden Pond" on page 14, I see a word that has two meanings: dove. *I can use the phrase* dove into the pond *to help me choose the correct meaning. That also helps me figure out the right way to say the word.*

Thoreau tried to get a close look at the loon, but the bird quickly dove into the pond.

Your Turn Use sentence clues to figure out the meanings of the following homographs in "A Life in the Woods."

felt, page 14 _____

wind, page 14 _____

CHECK IN 1 2 3 4

Ask and Answer Questions

When you read, you can ask yourself questions to monitor, or check, your understanding. Asking and then finding the answers to questions such as *What just happened?* or *Why did that happen?* will help you deepen your understanding of the text and gain knowledge. You can also ask and answer questions about the whole selection.

 FIND TEXT EVIDENCE

After you read the first paragraph of "A Life in the Woods" on page 13, you might ask yourself: *Why did Thoreau have to find a place of his own?* Reread the paragraph to find the answer.

Page 13

Into the Woods

Henry David Thoreau raised his pen to write, but the chatter of guests in the next room filled his ears. He stared at the page. "Concord, 1841" was all that he had written. How would he write a book with such noise in his family's house? Thoreau headed outside, shutting the door with **emphasis**. He would have to find a place of his own.

I read that Thoreau wondered how he could write a book with such noise in his family's house. From this I can infer that Thoreau needed to find a place of his own because the noise in his family's house made it impossible for him to write.

Your Turn Reread "Back to Concord" on page 15. Ask a question that will help you check your understanding. How can you find the answer?

_____

_____

CHECK IN 1 2 3 4

Primary and Secondary Sources

The selection "A Life in the Woods" is a narrative nonfiction text. Narrative nonfiction gives facts about real people and events. It tells a true story with a beginning, middle, and end. It may include both primary and secondary sources.

FIND TEXT EVIDENCE

I can tell that "A Life in the Woods" is narrative nonfiction. It gives facts about a real person, Henry David Thoreau, using primary and secondary sources. It also tells a story about how Thoreau was able to write a book about his experiences at Walden Pond.

Readers to Writers

One reason authors use primary sources such as journals, diaries, and letters is so the reading audience can hear directly from people who experienced the events firsthand. This makes the writing more interesting and helps the reader to understand the subject matter better. Good authors make sure that their primary sources are credible, or believable. How can you use this feature in your own writing?

Page 14

Cabin Life

Thoreau's move to the woods **indicated** that he liked to be alone. But Thoreau did not feel that way. "I have a great deal of company in my house," he wrote. Red squirrels woke him by running up and down the **sheer** sides of his cabin. A snowshoe hare lived in the **debris** under his cabin, thumping against the floorboards. A sparrow once perched on his shoulder. Thoreau recorded these experiences in his journal. How easily writing came to him with the beauty of nature around him!

On Walden Pond

Thoreau was a **naturalist**. He noticed the habits of animals. Each **encounter** showed him something new. One afternoon, Thoreau tried to get a close look at a loon, but the bird quickly dove into the pond. He knew loons could travel long distances under water, so he guessed where it would come up. But every time Thoreau paddled to one spot, the loon came up somewhere else and let out a call—a howling laugh. What a silly loon, Thoreau thought. But after a while, Thoreau felt as though the bird was laughing at him because he still could not catch up to it. Thoreau wrote in his journal:

His white breast, the stillness of the air, and the smoothness of the water were all against him. At length he uttered one of those prolonged howls, as if calling on the god of the loons to aid him, and immediately there came a wind from the east and rippled the surface, and filled the whole air with misty rain, and I was impressed.

WALDEN.

By HENRY D. THOREAU.

Thoreau published his book *Walden* in 1854.

Secondary Source

A secondary source, or account, retells or interprets information from a primary source.

Primary Source

A primary source provides firsthand information about a topic. Autobiographies, journals, and letters are examples.

COLLABORATE

Your Turn Reread the passage "Cabin Life" on page 14. Find a sentence that comes from a primary source. How is a primary source unique?

_____

_____

_____

_____

CHECK IN 1 2 3 4

Cause and Effect

Authors may organize information into a cause-and-effect text structure to explain how and why things happen. A **cause** is an event or action that makes something happen. An **effect** is what happens as the result of a cause. Sometimes signal words and phrases such as *because, so,* and *as a result* are used to link ideas and show cause-and-effect relationships.

FIND TEXT EVIDENCE

When I read the section "Into the Woods" from "A Life in the Woods" on page 13, I can look for signal words that show cause-and-effect relationships. I see the signal word because *in the sentence, "Because he and Thoreau shared the same interest in nature, Emerson decided to let Thoreau use part of this land."*

Cause	⟶	Effect
Emerson and Thoreau shared an interest in nature.	⟶	Emerson let Thoreau use his land.

Your Turn Reread "A Life in the Woods." Find cause-and-effect relationships and list them in your graphic organizer on page 21.

DenisTangneyJr/iStock/Getty Images

Quick Tip

If there are no signal words, you can use the following to help you identify cause and effect text structure:

Because of this:

_____

Thoreau did this:

_____

CHECK IN 1 ⟩ 2 ⟩ 3 ⟩ 4

Cause	→	Effect
	→	
	→	
	→	

My Goal: I can use text evidence to respond to narrative nonfiction.

Respond to Reading

COLLABORATE

Discuss the prompt below. Use your notes and text evidence to support your response.

How might Thoreau's life have been different had he not spent so much time in the woods?

Quick Tip

Use these sentence starters to organize ideas.

- *In the beginning, Thoreau felt . . .*
- *Thoreau's desire for change led him to . . .*
- *Thoreau discovered that nature . . .*

Readers to Writers

When you write about a text, it is important to use information from that text to support your ideas. Using text evidence helps your readers know that your response is appropriate. It also helps you to know whether or not you understand the text. If you can't find evidence to support your ideas, then you may need to revise your response.

CHECK IN 1 2 3 4

Experiencing Nature

COLLABORATE

Today, the National Park Service protects over 60 national parks so that we can visit and learn from nature. Follow the research process to create a map that promotes, or encourages, people to visit a national park. Your map can be drawn on paper or created digitally. Work collaboratively with a group.

Step 1 **Set a Goal** List a few national parks that interest you. Then choose one park to research.

Step 2 **Identify Sources** Use reliable print sources or websites, such as the National Park Service website, to find information about your park.

Step 3 **Find and Record Information** Find relevant information by focusing your search. Enter keywords about popular park attractions in a search engine. Take notes and cite your sources.

Step 4 **Organize and Synthesize Information** Create a rough sketch of your map by including features such as
- insets to show more detail of places in the park;
- symbols for attractions, roads, trails, and other places;
- a legend, or key, to identify these symbols.

Step 5 **Create and Present** Create a final map. After you finish, think about how you will present your map to the class.

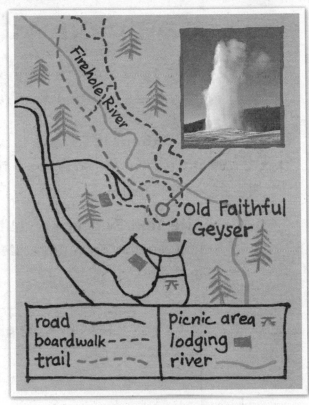

Old Faithful geyser erupts about every 94 minutes.

 Tech Tip

To create a digital map, you can use a mapmaking program. The National Park Service website also includes different kinds of maps of park roads, trails, and attractions.

CHECK IN 1 ⟩ 2 ⟩ 3 ⟩ 4

Lorcel/Shutterstock.com

*Literature Anthology:
pages 10–25*

Camping with the President

? How does the author help you visualize what President Roosevelt sees and hears at Yosemite?

Talk About It Reread **Literature Anthology** pages 16–17. Turn to a partner and discuss how the author describes what President Roosevelt experiences.

Cite Text Evidence What words and phrases help you create mental images about what President Roosevelt sees and hears? Write text evidence in the chart.

Text Evidence	What I Visualize

Write The author helps me visualize what Roosevelt sees and hears by

_____

_____

_____

_____

CHECK IN 1 2 3 4

Why is it significant that President Roosevelt decides to help John Muir?

 Talk About It Reread **Literature Anthology** page 19. Turn to your partner and discuss how President Roosevelt reacts to what John Muir tells him.

Cite Text Evidence How does President Roosevelt feel about the sequoia trees being cut down? Write text evidence in the chart.

 Evaluate Information

Evaluate, or decide, which details are important to understanding how Roosevelt feels about the sequoia trees being cut down. Evaluating the details you read will help you determine important ideas.

Text Evidence	What He Plans To Do

Write It is significant that Roosevelt decides to help Muir because

_____

_____

_____

_____

CHECK IN 1 > 2 > 3 > 4

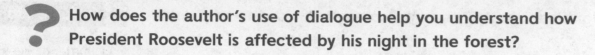

? How does the author's use of dialogue help you understand how President Roosevelt is affected by his night in the forest?

Talk About It Reread **Literature Anthology** pages 22–23. Turn to a partner and talk about what President Roosevelt said.

Cite Text Evidence What does President Roosevelt say that shows how he feels? Write text evidence in the web.

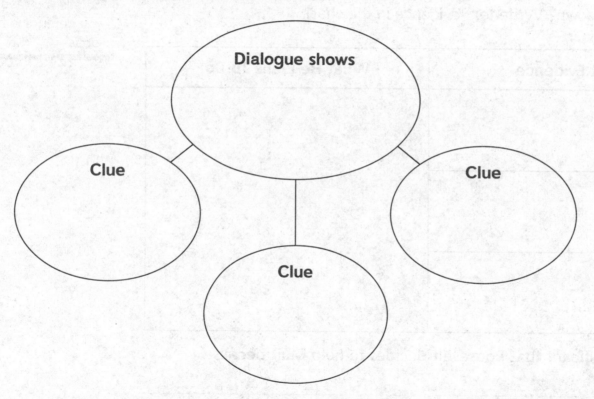

Dialogue shows

Clue

Clue

Clue

Quick Tip

President Roosevelt uses the word *bullier*. To understand what it means, read the words and sentences around this word. Thinking about Roosevelt's actions can also help you understand the word.

Make Inferences

Punctuation in dialogue can help you infer, or figure out, how the person speaking feels. Notice how often Roosevelt's dialogue ends with an exclamation mark. What kind of feelings do these marks express? Use what you know about exclamation marks and specific dialogue to help you infer how the president feels.

Write The author uses dialogue to help me understand that Roosevelt feels _____

_____

_____

CHECK IN 1 2 3 4

Respond to Reading

Discuss the prompt below. Use your notes and text evidence to support your ideas.

How did Roosevelt's feelings about nature drive his decisions and actions?

_____

_____

_____

_____

_____

_____

_____

_____

_____

_____

_____

_____

_____

Quick Tip

Use these sentence starters to organize your text evidence.

- *The author writes about what Roosevelt saw and heard because . . .*

- *Roosevelt decided to help Muir because . . .*

- *This helps me understand that Roosevelt . . .*

haveseen/Shutterstock.com

CHECK IN 1 2 3 4

A Walk with Teddy

1   "We left London on the
morning of June 9...Getting
off the train at Basingstoke,
we drove to the pretty, smiling
valley of the Itchen. Here we
tramped for three or four hours,
then again drove, this time to the edge of the New
Forest, where we first took tea at an inn, and then
tramped through the forest to an inn on its other
side, at Brockenhurst. At the conclusion of our
walk my companion made a list of the birds we
had seen...

2   The bird that most impressed me on my walk
was the blackbird. I had already heard nightingales
in abundance near Lake Como... but I had never
heard either the blackbird, the song thrush, or the
blackcap warbler; and while I knew that all three
were good singers, I did not know what really
beautiful singers they were. Blackbirds were very
abundant, and they played a prominent part in
the chorus which we heard throughout the day...
In its habits and manners the blackbird strikingly
resembles our American robin... "

Literature Anthology:
pages 28–31

Reread paragraphs 1 and 2. **Underline** words
and phrases that show what Theodore
Roosevelt learned about blackbirds.

Circle one sentence that tells Roosevelt's
opinion of blackbirds. Write it here:

_____

_____

_____

_____

_____

Make a mark beside each time Roosevelt
compares the blackbird to another bird
he knows. Talk with a partner about the
comparisons he makes and why.

A Man of Action

1   Roosevelt realized that seeing and hearing these birds in the wild gave him more information than any book. He could see the birds in action. He could hear their calls to each other. His experience revealed much about the birds of the country.

2   Roosevelt continued to travel throughout his life. He took every opportunity to study animals in the wild. But his travels also showed him that habitats needed to be protected. In his years as president, Roosevelt worked to preserve land. He established 150 national forests, 4 national parks, and 51 bird reservations. These sites continue to protect the nation's wildlife.

Elaine Mayes/Digital Vision/Getty Images

Reread paragraph 1 on page 29. **Circle** all the ways that Roosevelt gained information about birds.

Draw a box around what his experience taught him.

COLLABORATE

Reread paragraph 2. Look at the photograph and the caption. **Underline** the words that help you see how Roosevelt took action as president.

Talk with a partner about why "A Man of Action" is a good title for this section. Use your annotations and the photograph to support your response.

_____

_____

_____

_____

Roosevelt declared Crater Lake a national park. This lake is the deepest lake in the United States. It has a depth of 1,943 feet.

? How do the excerpts, photograph, and caption help you understand that Roosevelt's trip to England had a lasting impact on him?

Talk About It Reread the excerpt on page 29 and look at the photograph. Talk with a partner about the things Roosevelt did after his trip to England.

Cite Text Evidence Give examples of information about Roosevelt's experiences with nature. Use the web to record text evidence.

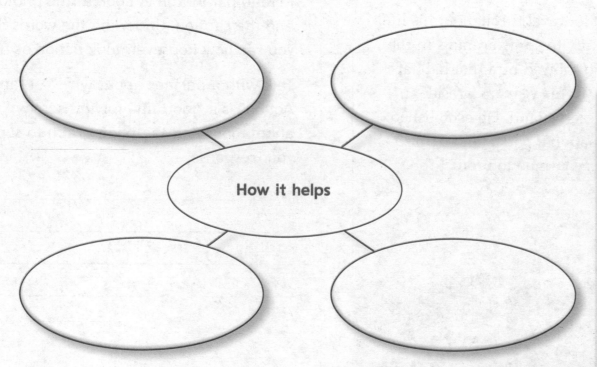

How it helps

Write I know Roosevelt's trip had an impact on his life because

_____

_____

_____

CHECK IN   1   2   3   4

Newman Mark/Prisma by Dukas Presseagentur GmbH/Alamy Stock Photo

Author's Perspective

In an autobiography, the author uses first-person point of view to tell about his or her own experience. In a biography, the author uses a third-person point of view to tell about someone else's experience. Authors use point of view to share their perspective, or attitude, about their subject or topic.

🔍 FIND TEXT EVIDENCE

In the "A Walk with Teddy" excerpts on pages 28–29, the author begins the story with Theodore Roosevelt's first-person point of view of his bird walk in England. Then the author switches to a third-person point of view to tell how this walk was important to Roosevelt.

"The bird that most impressed me on my walk was the blackbird."

Roosevelt realized that seeing and hearing these birds in the wild gave him more information than any book.

Your Turn Reread the rest of the second paragraph on page 28 and the paragraphs on page 29.

- What details help you understand the author's perspective about Roosevelt's walk? _____

_____

- Why do you think the author included Roosevelt's own words? _____

_____

CHECK IN 1 > 2 > 3 > 4 >

Readers to Writers

You can identify an author's perspective by paying attention to the author's word choice. What details do you notice in Roosevelt's first-person account? Think about how you might use this technique in your own writing.

? What do the photograph, caption, *Camping with the President,* and "A Walk with Teddy" help you understand about nature?

Alan and Sandy Carey/Getty Images

Talk About It Look at the photograph and read the caption. Talk with a partner about how it makes you feel and why.

Cite Text Evidence **Underline** the cause and effect of the Bald Eagle Protection Act noted in the caption. **Circle** three details in the photo that show how powerful and strong this bald eagle is. Think about how the authors use words and phrases to paint pictures of nature in the selections you read.

Write The photograph, caption, and the selections help me understand nature by _____

_____

_____

_____

_____

_____

_____

> ### Quick Tip
> Use details in the photograph to help you experience nature. Then think about the authors' messages about nature.

In 1940, the Bald Eagle Protection Act was passed to prevent bald eagles from going extinct. In 2007, the bird was no longer threatened because its population had greatly recovered.

CHECK IN 1 2 3 4

My Goal I know how experiencing nature can change the way people think about it.

Write a Public Service Announcement

Think about the texts you read about how experiencing nature changes the way people think and feel about it. Why is it important to experience nature?

1 Look at your Build Knowledge notes in your reader's notebook.

2 Write a public service announcement about why it is important to experience nature. Use evidence from the texts you read to support your ideas.

3 Be sure the message of your announcement is clear. Grab the reader's attention with a question or an interesting fact. Use new vocabulary words.

Think about what you learned in this text set. Fill in the bars on page 11.

Build Knowledge

Build Vocabulary

Write new words you learned about how we get the things we need. Draw lines and circles for the words you write.

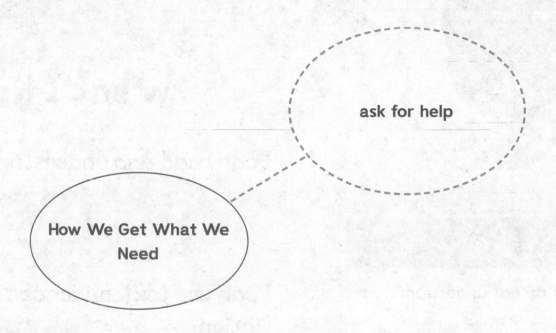

ask for help

How We Get What We Need

Go online to **my.mheducation.com** and read the "Clothing, Food, and Shelter" Blast. Think about the things that people need to survive. How could you help others in society get what they need? Then blast back your response.

Think about what you already know. Fill in the bars. There are no wrong answers here.

What I Know Now

I can read and understand realistic fiction.

| 1 | 2 | 3 | 4 |

I can use text evidence to respond to realistic fiction.

| 1 | 2 | 3 | 4 |

I know how people get the things they need.

| 1 | 2 | 3 | 4 |

Key	
1 =	I do not understand.
2 =	I understand but need more practice.
3 =	I understand.
4 =	I understand and can teach someone.

STOP You will come back to the next page later.

Think about what you learned. Fill in the bars. What helped you the most?

What I Learned

I can read and understand realistic fiction.

1   2   3   4

I can use text evidence to respond to realistic fiction.

1   2   3   4

I know how people get the things they need.

1   2   3   4

My Goal I can read and understand realistic fiction.

TAKE NOTES

As you read, make note of interesting words and important events.

_____

_____

_____

_____

_____

_____

_____

_____

_____

_____

_____

A Fresh Idea

Essential Question

How do we get the things we need?

Read about how one girl meets a need in her neighborhood.

One bright Saturday morning, Mali and her mom walked around the neighborhood. That is, her mom walked, but Mali ran, skipped, jumped over puddles, and visited the neighbors' dogs. Mali paused to look at the budding trees on her block. "I can't wait until summer," she said, "especially for Mrs. Fair's great tomatoes at her market stand." She pointed.

Mali's mom stood looking at the empty lot where the market set up every summer weekend. She looked at Mali. "Honey, Mrs. Fair told me last week that she had to close her stand. She's really getting too old to run it anymore."

Mali turned, stared, and put her hands on her hips. "But Mrs. Fair's stand can't close!" she said. "It's the only place in the neighborhood we can buy fresh, delicious tomatoes." Then she added, to show she wasn't being selfish, "Everyone needs fruits and vegetables for a healthy diet."

After they got home, Mali headed out to her backyard swing to think. "If only I could plant a garden," she thought, "but our yard is way too small." Just then, she noticed her neighbor, Mr. Taylor, looking at his daffodils. Mali knew he was thinking about how he had planted those flowers with his wife. This was the first spring since his wife had died, and Mali saw the sadness on his face. Then she had an idea.

Valerie Dacampo

FIND TEXT EVIDENCE

Read

Paragraphs 1–2

Reread

In paragraph 1, Mali is happy. In paragraph 2, she is upset. **Draw a box** around why her mood changes.

Paragraph 3

Context Clues

Circle the words that help you determine what *diet* means. Write its meaning.

Paragraph 4

Plot: Events

Underline the character introduced in paragraph 4. Is this before or after Mali thinks about her problem?

Reread

Author's Craft

How does the author use the relationship between Mali and Mr. Taylor to build the plot?

SHARED READ

FIND TEXT EVIDENCE

Read

Paragraphs 1–3

Reread

How can rereading the first three paragraphs help you understand and retell Mali's idea?

_____

_____

_____

_____

_____

_____

Paragraphs 4–6

Plot: Events

Underline three events that retell important elements of the story.

Reread

Author's Craft

How does the falling action show the changes in Mr. Taylor and Mali's relationship?

Mali cleared her throat, and Mr. Taylor looked up. Mali decided to walk over to the fence. "Hi, Mr. Taylor," she said. He waved, and turned away. "Wait!" Mali cried. Taking a **risk** while she still felt brave, she rushed to gather her thoughts: "Mr. Taylor, Mrs. Fair isn't doing her tomato stand anymore because she's getting old. So I'd like to grow tomatoes. I don't want to get in the way of your flowers, though. I mean, I really like tomatoes."

Suddenly, Mr. Taylor smiled. "Mali, I'm not sure what you're talking about, but you've made me smile. Reasons to smile have been **scarce** lately. What do you want to do?"

As Mr. Taylor listened, an idea came to him. "I still need a place to plant my flowers, but there's room for tomatoes. How about I make you a **loan?** I'll let you use a plot of land in my yard. I'll help you, and when your garden starts to **prosper,** you can repay me with a few tomatoes."

Mali and Mr. Taylor shook hands on this deal. "But first," Mr. Taylor said, "you'll have to make an investment by buying some tomato plants at the nursery."

Mali thought. "Well, I have some **savings** from my allowance, and I was saving to buy a computer game." She paused. "But I'd rather have tomatoes, so let's start right away!"

The next day, Mali bought all the tomato plants she could **afford.** Mr. Taylor taught Mali how to prepare the soil and place the plants. Finally, Mali placed stakes as supports in the ground to help hold the plants up. Mr. Taylor explained, "Once the tomatoes come, the heavy fruit makes the branches bend." Then all they could do was water, pull weeds, and wait.

When the fruit ripened, there were more juicy, red tomatoes than even Mali could have imagined. "There is no way I can eat all these," she realized. On Saturday, Mali and Mr. Taylor carried several crates of ripe tomatoes to the market, and by the day's end they had sold them all. "Not only did I get back the money I invested," said Mali, "but I also made a **profit** of twenty dollars!"

Mr. Taylor said, "Those are also your **wages!** You've earned that money."

Summarize

Use your notes to summarize what happened in the story and to describe the main characters.

Mali beamed and said, "Mr. Taylor, maybe you could sell some of your flowers, and we could run a market stand together!" Mr. Taylor, picturing a garden of zinnias and marigolds, was already looking forward to next summer.

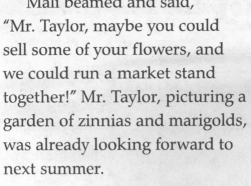

FIND TEXT EVIDENCE

`Read`

Paragraphs 1–2
Plot: Events

Underline what happens that changes Mali's original idea of growing tomatoes for herself.

Paragraph 3
Plot: Conflict and Resolution

Draw a box around what Mali says to Mr. Taylor in paragraph 3. How does the story end?

_____

_____

_____

_____

_____

_____

`Reread`

Author's Craft

What is the significance of Mr. Taylor "already looking forward to next summer"?

Vocabulary

Use the example sentences to talk with a partner about each word. Then answer the questions.

afford

Jill looked at the price tag to see if she could **afford** to buy the blouse.

Name something you would like to be able to afford.

_____

_____

loan

Lin asked her mom for a **loan** of five dollars.

When have you made a loan to someone?

_____

_____

profit

Jem made a **profit** of five dollars from selling lemonade.

When have you made a profit?

_____

_____

prosper

With enough care, a garden can **prosper**.

What other things help people to prosper?

_____

_____

risk

Firefighters take a great **risk** when they enter a burning building.

In what other jobs do people take a risk?

_____

_____

Build Your Word List Reread the first paragraph on page 41. Circle the word *imagined*. In your reader's notebook, use a word web to write more forms of the word. For example, write *imaginative*. Use an online or print dictionary to check for accuracy.

savings

Ray sets aside one dollar a week and puts it into his **savings**.

What would you do with some savings?

_____

_____

_____

scarce

Water can become **scarce** during hot, dry weather.

What is another word or phrase for _scarce_?

_____

_____

_____

wages

Sam earns **wages** for raking leaves every autumn.

What is a synonym for _wages_?

_____

_____

_____

Context Clues

Words and phrases in a sentence may help you figure out the meaning of an unfamiliar or multiple-meaning word. Sometimes clues may be in the form of synonyms, words with the same meanings, or antonyms, words with opposite meanings.

🔍 FIND TEXT EVIDENCE

I'm not sure what plot _means in the sentence_ "I'll let you use a plot of land in my yard." _But I can use the phrase_ "in my yard" _with the word_ "land" _to figure out that_ plot _means_ "a piece of ground."

I'll let you use a plot of land in my yard. I'll help you, and when your garden starts to prosper, you can repay me with a few tomatoes.

Your Turn Use sentence clues to figure out the meanings of the following words from "A Fresh Idea."

stakes, page 40 _____

_____

ripened, page 41 _____

_____

CHECK IN ▸ 1 〉 2 〉 3 〉 4 〉

Reread

When you read a story for the first time, you might find that some events or characters' relationships seem unclear. As you read "A Fresh Idea," stop and reread difficult parts of the story to make sure you understand them. Retell the events and analyze, or describe, the characters' relationships to check your understanding of the story.

FIND TEXT EVIDENCE

You may not be sure how Mali got her idea to grow a garden of her own with Mr. Taylor's help. Reread the fourth paragraph on page 39.

Page 39

Just then, she noticed her neighbor, Mr. Taylor, looking at his daffodils. Mali knew he was thinking about how he had planted those flowers with his wife. This was the first spring since his wife had died, and Mali saw the sadness on his face. Then she had an idea.

When I read, I see that Mr. Taylor knows how to plant gardens. He is also sad because his wife died. Mali got her idea after noticing Mr. Taylor's flowers and his sadness.

Your Turn Reread page 41. Discuss and retell why Mali decides to sell her tomatoes. Also tell what Mr. Taylor's actions show about his relationship with Mali. Remember to use the Reread strategy.

_____

_____

_____

CHECK IN 1 2 3 4

Plot: Conflict and Resolution

Realistic fiction is a made-up story that has characters who look and act like real people and often includes dialogue, or the words characters speak. It takes place in a setting that could be real and has a **plot**, or story events, that could really happen. A conflict, or problem, is introduced at the beginning of the story. The elements, or parts, of a plot include rising action, climax, falling action, and resolution.

Quick Tip

When you analyze a plot, you discuss the plot elements.

The **rising action** shows more about the main conflict, or problem. The **climax** is the turning point or high point of interest. The **falling action** is the events that happen after the climax and lead to the resolution. In the **resolution**, the conflict is resolved, and the story ends.

🔍 FIND TEXT EVIDENCE

I can tell that "A Fresh Idea" is realistic fiction. Details about the neighborhood show it could be a real place. The characters say and do things that real people might say and do. All the events could really happen.

Page 39

One bright Saturday morning, Mali and her mom walked around the neighborhood. That is, her mom walked, but Mali ran, skipped, jumped over puddles, and visited the neighbors' dogs. Mali paused to look at the budding trees on her block. "I can't wait until summer," she said, "especially for Mrs. Fair's great tomatoes at her market stand." She pointed.

Mali's mom stood looking at the empty lot where the market set up every summer weekend. She looked at Mali. "Honey, Mrs. Fair told me last week that she had to close her stand. She's really getting too old to run it anymore."

Mali turned, stared, and put her hands on her hips. "But Mrs. Fair's stand can't close!" she said. "It's the only place in the neighborhood we can buy fresh, delicious tomatoes." Then she added, to show she wasn't being selfish, "Everyone needs fruits and vegetables for a healthy diet."

After they got home, Mali headed out to her backyard swing to think. "If only I could plant a garden," she thought, "but our yard is way too small." Just then, she noticed her neighbor, Mr. Taylor, looking at his daffodils. Mali knew he was thinking about how he had planted those flowers with his wife. This was the first spring since his wife had died, and Mali saw the sadness on his face. Then she had an idea.

Plot
The plot is the sequence of events that make up a story.

Illustrations
Illustrations can give readers visual clues about characters, settings, and events.

Your Turn Analyze the plot elements in "Fresh Idea." How does the rising action lead to the climax? _____

_____

_____

CHECK IN 1 2 3 4

Plot: Events

Authors organize story events in a way that moves the plot forward. Each event leads to the next and reveals how the setting, characters, or conflict affect one another. You can analyze how these elements contribute to the plot by identifying the events at the beginning, middle, and end of a story.

 FIND TEXT EVIDENCE

On page 39 of "A Fresh Idea," I can read the sequence of events that leads to Mali's idea. The beginning of the story introduces Mali, her mom, and their neighborhood. Then we learn about Mali's problem.

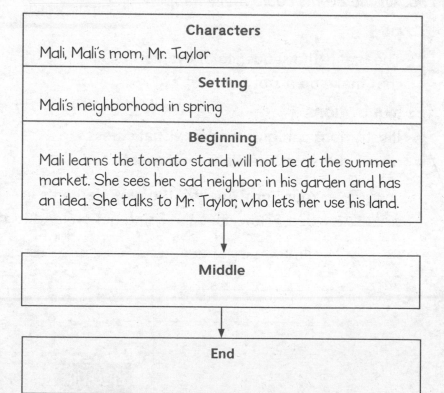

| **Characters** |
| Mali, Mali's mom, Mr. Taylor |
| **Setting** |
| Mali's neighborhood in spring |
| **Beginning** |
| Mali learns the tomato stand will not be at the summer market. She sees her sad neighbor in his garden and has an idea. She talks to Mr. Taylor, who lets her use his land. |

Middle

End

> **Quick Tip**
>
> Notice how characters think, act, behave, and respond to events. Their motivations and interactions advance, or move, the plot forward. The setting, or when and where the story takes place, also affects the plot.

 Your Turn Reread "A Fresh Idea." List events in the middle and end of the story in the graphic organizer on page 47. Select important details to show the sequence of events.

CHECK IN 1 2 3 4

Characters

Mali, Mali's mom, Mr. Taylor

Setting

Mali's neighborhood in spring

Beginning

Mali learns the tomato stand will not be at the summer market. Mali sees her sad neighbor in his garden and has an idea. She talks to Mr. Taylor, who lets her use his land.

↓

Middle

↓

End

Respond to Reading

COLLABORATE

Discuss the prompt below. Use your notes and text evidence to support your answer.

What does Mali and Mr. Taylor's relationship teach you?

_____

_____

_____

_____

_____

_____

_____

_____

_____

_____

_____

_____

_____

Quick Tip

Use these sentence starters to discuss the text and to organize ideas.

- *Mali and Mr. Taylor both feel . . .*

- *Mali and Mr. Taylor decide to help each other because . . .*

- *Mali and Mr. Taylor both benefit from the relationship by . . .*

Grammar Connections

Consider merging your sentences by combining ideas into compound sentences using words such as *and, but, or,* or *so.* For example: *Mali wants to plant a garden. Mali's yard is too small.* can be combined into: *Mali wants to plant a garden, but her yard is too small.*

CHECK IN 1 2 3 4

Meeting Needs

COLLABORATE

People farmed throughout the American colonies, but farming differed based on location. Follow the research process to create a compare/contrast chart that shows the differences between a New England, Middle, and Southern colony. Work collaboratively with a partner.

Step 1 **Set a Goal** Think about the information you need to research. Consider the impact that climate and soil conditions had on the types of crops farmers grew and the ways they planted and harvested. Write your ideas.

_____

Step 2 **Identify Sources** Evaluate multiple sources to make sure they provide reliable, or trusted, information. For example, primary and secondary sources from a museum or print encyclopedias are reliable. Generate and answer questions such as these.
- Is the source trustworthy?
- Does the source provide valid historical information?
- Does the source seem exaggerated or appear incomplete?

Step 3 **Find and Record Information** As you find relevant facts, take notes. Cite your sources.

Step 4 **Organize and Synthesize Information** Organize your notes into a compare/contrast chart. Consider adding photographs, illustrations, or maps. Keep your audience in mind as you revise your information.

Step 5 **Create and Present** Complete your chart. After you finish, you will present your work to the class.

Tech Tip

Skim (read quickly) and scan (search quickly) a digital text to look for information you need. A digital text, read on a computer, may have links you can click on for more information.

What might you do to answer questions you have about the information in a source?

_____

_____

_____

_____

_____

CHECK IN ▶ 1 ⟩ 2 ⟩ 3 ⟩ 4

One Hen

 What message is the author sending by writing about the future that Kojo dreams about?

Literature Anthology: pages 32–45

 Talk About It Reread the last five paragraphs on **Literature Anthology** page 34. Turn to your partner and talk about what Kojo's plans are.

Cite Text Evidence What words and phrases tell about Kojo's plan for the future? Write text evidence and tell why it's important to the story.

💡 **Evaluate Information**

One Hen takes place in Ghana. Ghana is located in West Africa, where there are many farming villages. How does the cultural setting affect Kojo?

Text Evidence	Why It's Important

Write The author uses Kojo's dreams to _____

_____

_____

CHECK IN ▸ 1 ▸ 2 ▸ 3 ▸ 4 ▸

How does the author organize the events in the story to help you understand how one hen impacts Kojo's life?

 Talk About It Reread **Literature Anthology** page 40. Turn to your partner and retell what is happening in Kojo's life.

Cite Text Evidence How is each event in Kojo's life connected to the one before it? Write text evidence.

Quick Tip

Retelling can help you better understand the story. When you retell, use text evidence, such as specific details, to help you maintain the story's meaning and the logical order of events.

```
┌─────────────────────────────────────┐
│                                     │
└─────────────────────────────────────┘
                  ↓
┌─────────────────────────────────────┐
│                                     │
└─────────────────────────────────────┘
                  ↓
┌─────────────────────────────────────┐
│                                     │
└─────────────────────────────────────┘
                  ↓
┌─────────────────────────────────────┐
│                                     │
└─────────────────────────────────────┘
```

Write The author helps me understand how one hen impacts Kojo's

life by _____

_____

_____

CHECK IN 1 2 3 4

? How do you know that Kojo's dream will continue to come true?

Talk About It Reread **Literature Anthology** page 43. Talk with a partner about why Kojo gives Adika a loan.

Cite Text Evidence What clue tells you that Kojo is always thinking about the future? Use the chart to record text evidence.

Cause		Effect
	→	
	→	

Write I know that Kojo's dream will continue because the author _____

_____

_____

_____

CHECK IN 1 2 3 4

Respond to Reading

COLLABORATE Discuss the prompt below. Use your notes and text evidence to support your response.

My Goal

I can use text evidence to respond to realistic fiction.

How does the characterization of Kojo help him succeed? Why was his outlook on life so signficant to the story?

_____

_____

_____

_____

_____

_____

_____

_____

_____

_____

_____

Quick Tip

Use these sentence starters to talk about and organize your text evidence.

- *Kojo's dreams are important because . . .*
- *The sequence of events in Kojo's life shows me that . . .*
- *Kojo's outlook on life is meaningful because . . .*

CHECK IN 1 2 3 4

Eureka/Alamy Stock Photo

Reading Between the Dots

Literature Anthology:
pages 48–51

1   "Brittany, you have so many library books in this house, it isn't funny!" my grandmother yelled from the living room. You would think 30 library books in the house wouldn't be a pain, right? Wrong. That's because these books were Braille books. For those of you who don't know, Braille is a raised-dot code, invented by Louis Braille, that blind or visually disabled individuals read using their fingers. Braille takes up a lot of room on a page. One book in print can be many volumes in Braille.

2   My work as a library volunteer started in the summer of 2008. The Baltimore public school system required all of its students to do community service before graduation. I decided to volunteer at my state library for the blind and physically handicapped.

3   On my first day, I made six Braille copies of a booklet. No, I didn't have to make all of those bumps by hand! Like other Braille documents and books, the booklet was typed on a computer. A special program converted the print file into a Braille file. Then a machine called a Braille embosser was hooked up to a computer and made six copies of the booklet in a matter of minutes.

Reread paragraph 1. **Underline** the sentence that explains what Braille is.

Reread paragraph 2. **Draw a box** around the text that explains why Brittany volunteered at the library.

COLLABORATE

Reread paragraph 3. Talk with a partner about how the author used a machine to make copies instead of doing it by hand. Write the text evidence here:

_____

_____

_____

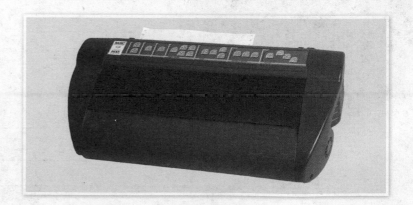

Bonnie Kamin/PhotoEdit

Louis Braille

[1] Louis Braille was born in France in 1809. He lost his vision at the age of three after a terrible accident. During his childhood, Braille attended the National Institute for Blind Youth in Paris. While there, he thought of ways to make reading easier for blind people. The method at that time was to read raised letters. But most blind people were unable to do this with much success.

[2] Braille came up with his idea for using raised dots instead after learning about a French officer in Napoleon's army who used a similar idea to help his soldiers communicate in the dark without making noise. By 1824, Braille had invented his raised dot code to help blind people read more efficiently. Over the years he improved his system, and it is still widely used today.

Reread paragraph 1. **Draw a box** around the text that tells how blind people used to read. Write it here:

_____

_____

_____

Reread paragraph 2. **Underline** the text that tells where Braille got his idea for using raised dots.

Talk with a partner about why Braille's system is still successful. **Circle** the text evidence that tells why it is still used today.

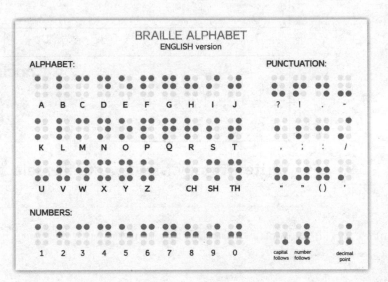

? What is Brittany Metts's purpose for writing this personal narrative? Use text evidence to support your answer.

Talk About It Reread the paragraphs on **Literature Anthology** pages 48 and 49. Talk with a partner about how Braille books are made.

Cite Text Evidence What are some details about Braille's system? How is Braille used? Use the chart to record text evidence.

Detail

↓

Detail

↓

Detail

↓

Conclusion

Write Brittany Metts wrote this selection to _____

_____

_____

CHECK IN 1 2 3 4

Chronology

A personal narrative describes events the author experienced. The narrative may be structured in a logical order such as chronology, or sequence of events. Sometimes, a personal narrative may start with an anecdote, or a brief story of some incident, to grab the reader's attention. The anecdote may entertain, inform, persuade, or inspire the reader.

 FIND TEXT EVIDENCE

Read **Literature Anthology** page 48 of "Reading Between the Dots." The first paragraph is an anecdote. Below is the beginning of the anecdote.

> "Brittany, you have so many library books in this house, it isn't funny!" my grandmother yelled from the living room. You would think 30 library books in the house wouldn't be a pain, right?

Your Turn Reread the first two paragraphs on pages 48–49.

• How does the author structure the text?

_____

_____

• What is the author's purpose for using an anecdote to begin her personal narrative? _____

_____

_____

Structuring a personal narrative in chronological order will help readers understand your experience. Focusing on parts of the experience in more detail will show readers what you think is most important. You may start a personal narrative with an anecdote.

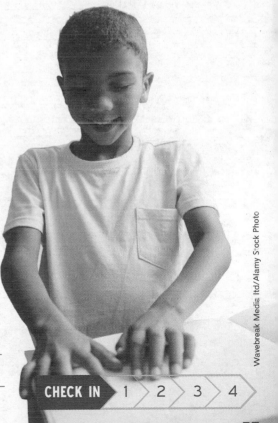

Wavebreak Media ltd/Alamy Stock Photo

CHECK IN ⟩ 1 ⟩ 2 ⟩ 3 ⟩ 4 ⟩

? How is the information in "Try Again" similar to the information in *One Hen* and "Reading Between the Dots?" How does this information help you understand how we get the things we need?

Talk About It Read the poem. Talk with a partner about the information you inferred. Discuss what the poet wants you to know.

Cite Text Evidence Reread the poem. **Circle** the phrase that is repeated. **Underline** words and phrases that tell what would happen if you follow the poet's advice. This is the effect. **Draw a box** around the cause. Compare this cause and effect with the causes and effects in the selections you read.

Write The poem and the selections help me understand that _____

_____

_____

_____

_____

_____

_____

_____

_____

Andrew Unangst/Photographer's Choice/Getty Images

> ### Quick Tip
>
> When you compare ideas, you show how they are the same. To help you compare ideas in the readings, think about how one event causes another to happen in *One Hen* and "Reading Between the Dots." Then do the same for "Try Again."

Try Again

If you find your task is hard,
    Try again;
Time will bring you your reward,
    Try again.
All that other folks can do,
With your patience should not you?
Only keep this rule in view—
    Try again.

— Anonymous

CHECK IN 〉 1 〉 2 〉 3 〉 4 〉

My Goal I know how people get the things they need.

Create an Award

Many people you read about figured out how to get the things they needed. What are some character traits they share? Create an award that honors these character traits and inspires others to accomplish their goals.

1 Look at your Build Knowledge notes in your reader's notebook.

2 Draw your award. Think of how you could represent the character traits you wish to honor.

3 Write a paragraph that describes how to nominate someone for the award. Use examples from the texts you read. Use new vocabulary words.

Think about what you learned in this text set. Fill in the bars on page 37.

Build Knowledge

Essential Question

What are the positive and negative effects of new technology?

Build Vocabulary

Write new words you learned about some positive or negative effects of new technology. Draw lines and circles for the words you write.

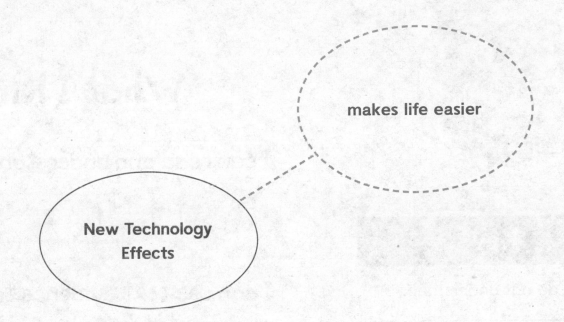

makes life easier

New Technology Effects

Go online to **my.mheducation.com** and read the "Riding Technology's Rollercoaster!" Blast. Think about your experiences with technology. How would you describe them? Then blast back your response.

Think about what you already know. Fill in the bars. You'll keep learning more.

What I Know Now

I can read and understand argumentative text.

1 > 2 > 3 > 4

I can use text evidence to respond to argumentative text.

1 > 2 > 3 > 4

I know the positive and negative effects of new technology.

1 > 2 > 3 > 4

Key	
1 =	I do not understand.
2 =	I understand but need more practice.
3 =	I understand.
4 =	I understand and can teach someone.

STOP You will come back to the next page later.

What I Learned

I can read and understand argumentative text.

1 > 2 > 3 > 4

I can use text evidence to respond to argumentative text.

1 > 2 > 3 > 4

I know the positive and negative effects of new technology.

1 > 2 > 3 > 4

My Goal I can read and understand argumentative text.

TAKE NOTES

As you read, make note of interesting words and important information.

TIME for **KiDS**

Essential Question

? **What are the positive and negative effects of new technology?**

Read two different perspectives about how technology affects kids.

Blend Images - JGI/Jamie Grill/Brand X Pictures/Getty Images

Are Electronic Devices Good for Us?

Plugged In

Kids need to spend time using electronic devices.

Do you love to surf the Internet, listen to music, text, and talk on a cell phone? You are not alone. A recent study has some surprising news: Kids in the United States between the ages of 8 and 18 spend seven and a half hours a day on electronic devices. These include computers, smart phones, and video games. Some adults try to **advance** the idea that these devices waste kids' time. However, some research surveys say this idea is inaccurate. In fact, the **data** show that technology can benefit kids.

Critics say that kids who stare at computers and TVs all day do not get enough exercise. The facts stand in **counterpoint** to this belief. One study compared kids who use media a lot to those who do not.

The "heavy" media users actually spent more time in physical activity than "light" media users.

One study by the National Institutes of Health says that action video games may help increase kids' visual attention. In addition, using interactive media can give kids good structure for learning. It can also help them learn to switch tasks effectively. Kids also need to use the Web to **access** information. Many argue that learning to use the Web responsibly sharpens kids' **reasoning** abilities.

Today's world is wired, and not just for fun. The jobs of the future depend on kids who plug in!

A Source of News for Teens

For the latest news, teens used to rely on newspapers, television, and magazines. See how many teens now get their news online.

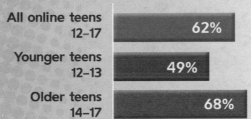

All online teens 12–17	62%
Younger teens 12–13	49%
Older teens 14–17	68%

FIND TEXT EVIDENCE

Read

Paragraph 1
Author's Claim

Circle the author's claim about electronic devices.
Underline the sentence that is opposite of the author's claim. How does the author use a fact against this opposite claim?

_____

_____

Paragraphs 2–4
Reread

Draw a box around the supporting evidence about visual attention that supports the author's claim.

Reread
Author's Craft

Why did the author include the sidebar graph "A Source of News for Teens"?

FIND TEXT EVIDENCE

Read

▼
Paragraphs 1–2

Author's Claim

Underline the author's claim about electronic media. What is the author's argument in the second paragraph?

_____

_____

Graphs

Draw a box around the pie graph that shows the lowest percentage of good grades.

Synthesize Information

What conclusion can you draw about media use?

_____

_____

Reread

Author's Craft

How does the author support his or her argument?

COUNTERPOINT

Tuned Out

Electronic media is harming kids.

Are kids tuning out by tuning in to electronic devices? An alarming report states that electronic media use has continued to grow over the past decade, aided by the increase in mobile phone use among teenagers. About 25 percent of teenagers consider themselves "constantly connected" to the Internet. Nearly 6 out of 10 kids get their first cell phone between the ages of 10–11. Are these devices harmless or hurtful to the well-being of young people? A close **analysis** of several studies shows that there are plenty of disadvantages to these devices.

The Internet is supposed to be a great tool for learning. Do kids who love computers do better in the classroom? To **cite** one report, access to electronic devices does not automatically bring high marks in school. See the graphs below.

The Effect of Media Use on Grades

These pie graphs show how the use of media affects grades.

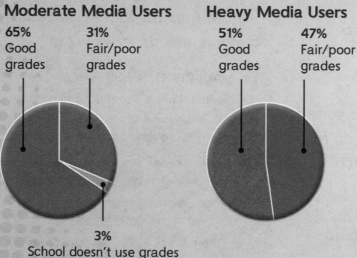

Moderate Media Users
65% Good grades   **31%** Fair/poor grades   **3%** School doesn't use grades

Heavy Media Users
51% Good grades   **47%** Fair/poor grades

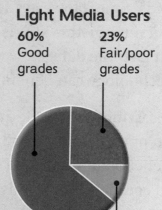

Light Media Users
60% Good grades   **23%** Fair/poor grades   **10%** School doesn't use grades

The effects of using electronic devices on kids will continue to be studied. These devices seem to be here to stay.

Some argue that the devices get kids involved and help them make friends. Claims like these are incorrect. A study done by the Pew Research Center discusses teenagers' use of online social networks. Teens use social media to keep in touch with friends they already have, not to make new ones. In addition, trying to meet people online can be dangerous.

There are other serious **drawbacks** to new technology. One issue is multitasking, or trying to do many tasks at the same time. Is it possible to do more than one task at a time well? Some studies say kids' thinking improves when they do several tasks at once. Still, experts point out that much more research needs to be done on this.

New electronic devices hit stores every year. Kids should know that there is more to life than what they see on a screen.

Summarize

Use your notes and the graphs to summarize each part of "Are Electronic Devices Good for Us?"

Thomas Barwick/Iconica/Getty Images

FIND TEXT EVIDENCE

Read

Paragraph 1
Greek and Latin Prefixes
The prefix *in-* sometimes means "not." What does the word *incorrect* mean?

Paragraph 2
Reread
Draw a box around what experts think about multitasking.

Paragraph 3
Author's Claim
Underline the author's argument in the last paragraph.
Who is the intended audience for this text?

Reread

Author's Craft

How does the author address and refute any counterargument?

Vocabulary

Use the example sentences to talk with a partner about each word. Then answer the questions.

access

Brad had to use a key to **access** the locked room.

How do you access information on a computer?

_____

_____

advance

Many people have marched to **advance** people's rights.

What would you do to advance a cause you believed in?

_____

_____

Build Your Word List Pick a word you found interesting in the selection you read. Look up the definition and the word's origin, the language the word comes from, in a print or online dictionary. Write the word and its definition and origin in your reader's notebook.

analysis

Karina used a magnifying glass to make a careful **analysis** of a seashell.

How do you do an analysis of information for a report?

_____

_____

cite

When doing research, it is important to identify and **cite** sources of information.

What sources might you cite when writing a report about a country?

_____

_____

counterpoint

One critic's positive review was in **counterpoint** to another's bad review.

What opinion have you had in counterpoint to that of a friend?

_____

_____

data

The students gathered **data** as they measured the growing plants' heights.

What data would you need to write a weather report?

_____

_____

_____

drawbacks

Fewer seats and a small trunk are **drawbacks** of a small car.

What are some drawbacks to going on a hike without the right equipment?

_____

_____

_____

reasoning

James used his **reasoning** skills before deciding on his next chess move.

What other situations require good reasoning?

_____

_____

Greek and Latin Prefixes

Prefixes are added to the beginnings of words and change their meanings. Prefixes that come from ancient Greek and Latin, such as *dis-, in-, tele-,* and *multi-,* are common in many English words. Prefixes can help you figure out an unfamiliar word's meaning.

🔍 FIND TEXT EVIDENCE

On page 66 of "Tuned Out," I can use prefixes to figure out the meaning of disadvantages. Dis- *means "opposite."* Advantages *means "qualities that help."* Disadvantages *must mean "harmful qualities."*

> A close analysis of several studies shows that there are plenty of disadvantages to these devices.

Your Turn Use Greek and Latin prefixes to define words from "Plugged In" and "Tuned Out."

Greek prefix: *tele-* = at a distance

television, *page 65* _____

_____

Latin prefix: *multi-* = many

multitasking, *page 67* _____

CHECK IN ▶ 1 ⟩ 2 ⟩ 3 ⟩ 4

Reread

Rereading a text—including opening and closing paragraphs—can help clarify points an author makes. It can help you monitor, or check, your comprehension of how ideas are presented and supported by an author. Rereading can also lead you to answer questions when your understanding of the text breaks down.

Quick Tip

Fill out a two-column graphic organizer as you reread "Are Electronic Devices Good for Us?" You can compare each author's ideas and decide if the conclusions are similar or different.

 FIND TEXT EVIDENCE

When I reread the end of the opening paragraphs of "Plugged In" on page 65 and "Tuned Out" on page 66, I can better understand what the different authors will be writing about.

Pages 65 and 66

Plugged In
In fact, the **data** show that technology can benefit kids.

Tuned Out
A close **analysis** of several studies shows that there are plenty of disadvantages to these devices.

The author of "Plugged In" says technology can benefit kids. The author of "Tuned Out" discusses disadvantages of technology. Rereading helps me see different ideas the authors are making.

 Your Turn Reread the conclusions of "Plugged In" and "Tuned Out." How are they similar or different? _____

_____

_____

CHECK IN 1 2 3 4

Headings and Graphs

"Plugged In" and "Tuned Out" are examples of argumentative text. Both include reasons and evidence that support a claim, or an argument. Authors of argumentative texts may address a counterargument, or opposite claim, and use facts to say why it may be incorrect. Text features such as headings and graphs may add support for an argument.

FIND TEXT EVIDENCE

I can tell that "Plugged In" on page 65 is argumentative text. The opening paragraph clearly states an argument. The second paragraph cites a study that supports the author's argument. A graph adds more support.

Page 65

Are Electronic Devices Good for Us?

Plugged In

Kids need to spend time using electronic devices.

Do you love to surf the Internet, listen to music, text, and talk on a cell phone? You are not alone. A recent study has some surprising news: Kids in the United States between the ages of 8 and 18 spend seven and a half hours a day on electronic devices. These include computers, smart phones, and video games. Some adults try to advance the idea that these devices waste kids' time. However, some research surveys say this idea is inaccurate. In fact, the data show that technology can benefit kids.

Critics say that kids who stare at computers and TVs all day do not get enough exercise. The facts stand in counterpoint to this belief. One study compared kids who use media a lot to those who do not.

The "heavy" media users actually spent more time in physical activity than "light" media users.

One study by the National Institutes of Health says that action video games may help increase kids' visual attention. In addition, using interactive media can give kids good structure for learning. It can also help them learn to switch tasks effectively. Kids also need to use the Web to access information. Many argue that learning to use the Web responsibly sharpens kids' reasoning abilities.

Today's world is wired, and not just for fun. The jobs of the future depend on kids who plug in!

A Source of News for Teens
For the latest news, teens used to rely on newspapers, television, and magazines. See how many teens now get their news online.

All online teens 12–17	62%
Younger teens 12–13	49%
Older teens 14–17	68%

Headings

A heading tells what a section of text is mainly about.

Graphs

A graph compares two or more quantities of something. Bars or sections show differences in amount. Labels identify the graph's main features.

COLLABORATE

Your Turn List three parts of the bar graph on page 65 of "Plugged In."

_____

_____

_____

CHECK IN 1 2 3 4

Author's Claim

An **author's claim,** or argument, tells the author's opinion on a topic or idea. Reasons and details, such as facts, figures, and examples, help to develop the claim. To identify a claim, look for the reasons and evidence for or against an idea or topic that support the author's argument.

Quick Tip

Pay attention to the author's word choice in an argumentative text. Words such as *don't* or *disadvantage* help readers identify and understand the author's argument.

🔍 FIND TEXT EVIDENCE

In "Plugged In" on page 65, I can identify the author's claim: "Kids need to spend time using electronic devices." The author supports this claim with evidence about exercise and learning. Finally, the author argues that technology creates the jobs of the future.

Details	Author's Claim
Users get exercise.	The author supports kids using electronic devices.
Helps kids' visual attention.	
Helps users with learning.	
These are jobs of the future.	

Your Turn Reread the counterpoint, "Tuned Out," on pages 66 and 67. Find details that support the author's argument and list them in the graphic organizer on page 73. Summarize the details to identify the author's claim.

CHECK IN ⟩ 1 ⟩ 2 ⟩ 3 ⟩ 4 ⟩

Details	Author's Claim

Respond to Reading

COLLABORATE

Discuss the prompt below. Use your notes and text evidence to support your answer.

Which author do you think has the more convincing argument? Cite text evidence to support your answer.

_____

_____

_____

_____

_____

_____

_____

_____

_____

_____

Quick Tip

Use these sentence starters to paraphrase the text as you discuss and organize ideas.

- *The first author cites a study to show that . . .*

- *In contrast, the second author believes that . . .*

- *Each author supports arguments with . . .*

Grammar Connections

Check your writing for comma splices. A comma splice is when two independent clauses are combined into one sentence with only a comma. For example, *Teens text too much, they should put their phones down.* should be *Teens text too much. They should put their phones down.*

CHECK IN 1 2 3 4

Technology

COLLABORATE

Many people have different viewpoints about technology. Follow the research process to prepare a debate. A debate is an organized discussion between two people or teams. Work collaboratively in groups to debate the positive and negative effects of a specific kind of technology.

Step 1 **Set a Goal** In groups of four, decide on the kind of technology you wish to research. Then, divide into two teams. One team will argue for a position, and the other will argue against it. Decide which team will take which position.

Step 2 **Identify Sources** As a team, identify websites or print sources that would help you find the main points for your position.

Step 3 **Find and Record Information** Research facts that support your position. Address points the opposing side may make. Cite your sources so that you can refer to them during the debate.

Step 4 **Organize and Synthesize Information** Analyze the information you gathered. Is your position clear? How will you respond to counterpoints? Revise your notes as needed.

Step 5 **Create and Present** After you complete your preparations, your group will debate in front of the class. Make sure to follow the rules of the debate.

Debate Format

• One team presents an argument that supports its position.

• The opposing team states its position.

• Each team then takes turns addressing the other team's arguments.

• Each team summarizes its position and closes with why their position is best.

The list above shows a brief outline for a debate.

What do you think is one important rule for a debate? Write it here.

_____

_____

_____

CHECK IN 1 2 3 4

The Future of Transportation

Literature Anthology:
pages 52–55

? **Reread "Autos Advance." How does the author's use of facts strengthen the argument?**

Talk About It Reread **Literature Anthology** page 53. Turn to your partner and discuss how the author compares modern cars and public transportation. Describe how the author uses literal language to support his or her claim.

Cite Text Evidence What words and phrases help you understand the author's argument? Write text evidence to support the claim.

Public Transportation	Cars

Quick Tip

When you discuss specific ideas in a text, you talk about how they are important to the text's meaning. In an argumentative text, some ideas support the author's claim. Knowing why the author included specific ideas can help you understand his or her perspective.

Write The author's argument is supported because _____

_____

? **How do the text features help you understand how the author of "The Rail Way" feels about public transportation?**

Talk About It Look at the features on **Literature Anthology** pages 54–55. Talk with your partner about how the features support the author's argument.

Cite Text Evidence What new and persuasive information did you learn by using the features? Write the evidence here.

Headings	Photographs	Captions

Write The author uses features to _____

_____

_____

Quick Tip

Sometimes authors use punctuation to emphasize their perspective. For example, the second heading on page 55 is "Speed Thrills!" Think about how the exclamation mark expresses how the author feels about high-speed trains.

Evaluate Information

Authors of argumentative texts often include a counterargument and then use facts against the argument. What is one counterargument the author included in "Speed Thrills!" How did he or she refute it?

CHECK IN 1 2 3 4

Respond to Reading

Discuss the prompt below. Use your notes and text evidence to support your ideas.

What is your opinion about transportation and technology? What reasons and evidence influenced your opinion the most?

_____

_____

_____

_____

_____

_____

_____

_____

_____

_____

_____

Quick Tip

Use these sentence starters to retell details in a way that maintains meaning about the texts and to cite text evidence.

• *In their arguments, each author . . .*

• *This helps me determine that . . .*

CHECK IN   1   2   3   4

narvikk/E+/Getty Images

Getting From Here to There

1 Passengers are not the only ones moving along these days. Transportation technology is moving along, too. Cars and trains are changing at a rapid pace. These advances may offer more ways of getting around in the future.

The Ways People Commute

2 While transportation researchers may count train passengers or the number of cars passing a toll, a survey is another way experts collect data. A government survey analysis showed most people get to work by personal vehicle. Some people interpret this to mean it is the preferred way to travel. Improving public transportation could change that.

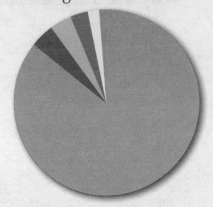

■ Car, truck, or van	86%
■ Biked or walked	4%
☐ Worked from home	4%
■ Bus	3%
☐ Railroad or subway	2%
☐ Other	1%

Source: U.S. Census Bureau, American Community Survey, *Commuting in the United States: 2009*, Table 1.

Literature Anthology:
pages 56–57

Reread paragraph 1. **Underline** the sentence that shows how the author feels about transportation technology. **Draw a box** around the sentence in paragraph 2 that relates to information in the pie chart.

COLLABORATE

Look at the pie chart. Talk with a partner about what the chart shows. How do you know which is the most popular way people commute? **Circle** the clue.

Draw an arrow to the least popular way people commute.

Chuck Eckert/Alamy Stock Photo

? How does the author help you understand how data can support improvements in transportation?

 Talk About It Reread the excerpt on page 79 and look at the pie chart. Talk with a partner about how the author's use of a chart helps get a point across.

Cite Text Evidence How does the pie chart help make technical information easier to understand? Write evidence in the web below.

Quick Tip

The chart on page 79 contains a list, or key. The key helps you to understand the information in the pie chart. What would happen if the author did not include the key?

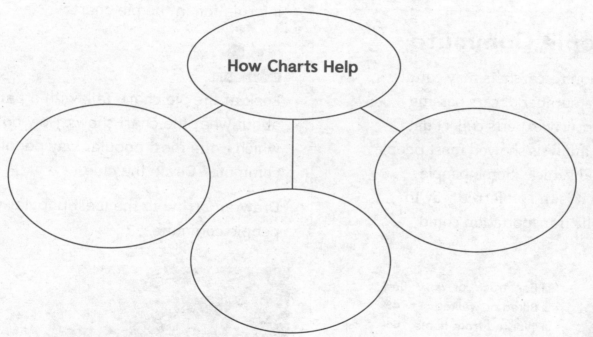

How Charts Help

 Make Inferences

The last entry in the key is "Other." Think about the first five entries. What other forms of transportation are missing from this key? Use what you know about transportation and commuting to infer what "Other" could mean.

Write The author's use of features helps me understand _____

_____

_____

Author's Purpose

An **author's purpose** is the reason the author writes. This purpose may be to persuade, inform, or entertain. In order to accomplish the purpose, an author thinks about the intended audience or reader. An author may use data when writing to inform or when writing to support a claim.

 FIND TEXT EVIDENCE

On page 79, the author expresses support for advances in transportation technology by saying that such advances may provide more transportation choices in the future. Future developments are important to readers.

> Transportation technology is moving along, too. Cars and trains are changing at a rapid pace. These advances may offer more ways of getting around in the future.

 Your Turn Reread the text on page 79 in the section "The Ways People Commute."

- Based on the data, what do some people conclude about personal vehicles? _____

_____

- Why does the author think the data about cars, trucks, and vans might change?_____

_____

Stay consistent with your opinion throughout your writing. Use supporting evidence when presenting information. Use logical, convincing facts to support a claim. Also include counterarguments, or opposing arguments, and use facts to refute them.

CHECK IN 1 2 3 4

? **How are the song lyrics about transportation similar to the information in the selections** *The Future of Transportation* **and "Getting from Here to There"?**

Talk About It Read the song lyrics for "Down Yonder." Talk with a partner about what the lyrics mean. Compare what they have in common with the selections about the positive or negative effects of transportation. When you compare ideas, you look to see how they are similar.

Cite Text Evidence In the song lyrics, **circle** phrases that tell how the songwriter feels about train travel. **Underline** clues that show why the songwriter feels this way.

Write The song lyrics and the selections are similar because _____

_____

_____

_____

_____

_____

_____

_____

_____

Down Yonder

Railroad train, railroad train,
  hurry some more;
Put a little steam on just like
  never before.
Hustle on, bustle on, I've got
  the blues,
Yearning for my Swanee
  shore.
Brother if you only knew, you'd
  want to hurry up, too.

— L. Wolfe Gilbert, 1921.

CHECK IN 1 2 3 4

My Goal I know the positive and negative effects of new technology.

Write a Top Five List

Think about the texts you read about how technology affects our lives. Write a list of the top five reasons. Rate these reasons from the least positive reason to the most positive reason.

1 Look at your Build Knowledge notes in your reader's notebook.

2 Start with number five. Place the least positive reason at number five and rate them all the way to one. Number one is the most positive. Be sure to use evidence from the texts you read.

3 Then write a paragraph explaining your reasons. Use new vocabulary words.

Think about what you learned in this text set. Fill in the bars on page 63.

Think about what you already know. Fill in the bars. Meeting your goals may take time.

What I Know Now

I can write an argumentative essay.

| 1 | 2 | 3 | 4 |

I can synthesize information from four sources.

| 1 | 2 | 3 | 4 |

Key

1 = I do not understand.

2 = I understand but need more practice.

3 = I understand.

4 = I understand and can teach someone.

What I Learned

I can write an argumentative essay.

I can synthesize information from four sources.

WRITE TO SOURCES

You will answer an argumentative prompt using sources and a rubric.

ANALYZE THE RUBRIC

A rubric tells you what needs to be included in your writing.

Purpose, Focus, and Organization
Read the second bullet. How should an argument be presented?

An argument _____

_____

_____

Evidence and Elaboration
Read the second bullet. What is the connection between evidence and the argument?

_____

_____

_____

Evidence and Elaboration
Underline the word or words in the second bullet that tell you where the evidence comes from.

Argumentative Writing Rubric

Purpose, Focus, and Organization • Score 4

- stays focused on the purpose, audience, and task
- **makes a claim that clearly supports a perspective**
- uses transitional strategies, such as words and phrases, to connect ideas
- presents ideas in a logical progression, or order
- begins with a strong introduction and ends with a strong conclusion

Evidence and Elaboration • Score 4

- effectively supports the claim with logical reasons
- has strong examples of relevant evidence, or supporting details, from multiple sources
- uses elaborative techniques, such as examples, definitions, and quotations from sources
- expresses interesting ideas clearly using precise language
- uses appropriate academic and domain-specific language
- uses different sentence structures

Turn to page 236 for the complete Argumentative Writing Rubric.

Make a Claim

Present a Strong Claim A strong claim clearly states an opinion about a topic. An opinion tells the author's perspective, or attitude, and beliefs about a topic. Read the paragraph below. The claim is highlighted.

What does the claim tell you about the topic of the essay?

> **People should visit the best of Florida's beautiful landscapes, such as the Panhandle.** Photographers can aim their cameras at the crystal-blue waters of the Gulf Islands National Seashore. Naturalists can observe herons in the grassy water. They should watch quietly when they see herons. Campers can hike on the Florida National Scenic Trail. Truly, all visitors will enjoy the Panhandle's natural beauty.

_____

_____

_____

Perspective When authors express their claims, or arguments, they are arguing for or against an idea. They convince their audience to support their claim with strong relevant evidence such as facts and details. These facts and details reveal the author's perspective.

Read the paragraph above. Cross out a piece of evidence that does NOT strongly support the author's perspective.

Audience

Writers have an audience in mind when they write. They make choices about what facts and details to include based on their audience. Reread the paragraph on the left. Who is the audience?

ANALYZE THE STUDENT MODEL

Paragraph 1

Read the first paragraph of Dario's essay. The claim is highlighted.

What is the topic of Dario's essay?

_____

_____

_____

Paragraph 2

Examples of evidence can be quotations or paraphrased words from sources.

Underline an example of evidence Dario cites in this paragraph. How does this example of evidence support his argument? _____

_____

_____

_____

Student Model: Argumentative Essay

Dario responded to the Writing Prompt: _Write an argumentative essay to present to your class. Answer the question: Should people experience nature through ecotourism?_ Read Dario's essay below.

1   According to the International Ecotourism Society, ecotourism is "responsible travel to natural areas that conserves the environments and improves the well-being of local people." Some people think that we should travel long distances to experience nature. People pay a lot of money and use a lot of energy for ecotourism. However, close to my own home, I can see turtles, snakes, frogs, birds, swamps, marshes, trees, and a creek. Just as I don't need to travel far to experience nature, most people do not need to travel far either. Since ecotourism can harm the environment, I urge people to experience nature in their local areas.

2   Research has shown that ecotourism can harm the environment. "A Green Vacation Is Not a Dream Vacation" tells about the environmental scientist Dr. Andrea Smith. She warns about the dangers of ecotourism. She says that more people means more hotels and roads, which are all dependent upon shipments from the mainland. The article says, "Shipments increase the risk of invasive species that threaten fragile ecosystems." This means that shipments

could bring in animals and plants that hurt the existing environment. In addition, a pie chart printed in "The Impact of Ecotourism" shows that transportation makes up 28 percent of the gases that cause pollution and damage the environment. Almost one-third of the pollution is caused by people traveling. We shouldn't add to this pollution that hurts nature.

3   People don't need to travel far and be adventurous to experience nature. As I pointed out, I can visit nature practically in my backyard. What about people who don't live as close to nature as I do? Even they can find nature in parks, in the trees on the street, or the birds in the air. When we go to Jacksonville, my family and I can look at the stars at night or the clouds during the day. We can examine bugs and birds. The article "The Impact of Ecotourism" introduces the idea of "staycations," which is "staying where you are and experiencing home in a new, relaxed way." What kind of nature might people discover if they stay in their own habitats?

4   For these reasons, people should not experience nature through ecotourism. They should see their own neighborhoods, homes, and parks with fresh eyes before harming fragile people, animals, and plants in distant places.

monkeybusinessimages/iStock/Getty Images

Paragraph 2
Circle an example of a transitional word or phrase Dario uses to connect his ideas.

Paragraph 3
Dario states a counterargument, or an opposite claim, to refute an argument. **Underline** his counterargument. How does his counterargument support his claim?

_____

_____

_____

_____

Paragraph 4
Draw a box around the transitional words that link his conclusion with the body of his essay.

Apply the Rubric

With a partner, use the rubric on page 86 to discuss why Dario scored a 4 on his essay.

Analyze the Prompt

Writing Prompt

Write an argumentative essay to present to your class. Answer the question: Should Florida's government use funds to protect natural lands or to develop land?

Purpose, Audience, and Task Reread the writing prompt. What is your purpose for writing? My purpose is to _____

_____

Who will your audience be? My audience will be _____

_____

What type of writing is the prompt asking for? _____

_____

Set a Purpose for Reading Sources Asking questions about whether Florida's government should use funds to develop land or protect its natural lands will help you figure out your purpose for reading. It also helps you understand what you already know about the topic. Before you read the passage set about what Florida should do, write a question here.

_____

_____

_____

Read the following passage set.

LANDMARK DEAL APPROVED!

1   According to research, Florida's population will increase by 5.6 million people by 2030. Osceola County officials approved Deseret Ranch's deal to turn 290,000 acres of ranchland into a new city that would house millions by 2080. **Deseret Ranch's proposal to develop land is absolutely critical to meet this massive growth in Florida's population.**

2   Erik Jacobsen, Deseret Ranch's general manager, says that turning the land into residential and commercial development is practical. He says it's his responsibility to help plan for inevitable growth.

3   Deseret Ranch and county officials will set aside protected natural areas. According to an official study, the development will not bring adverse impacts to the wilderness, wetlands, or wildlife.

4   The need for land preservation is essential. But it is imperative to be prepared to manage urban growth. This deal is necessary.

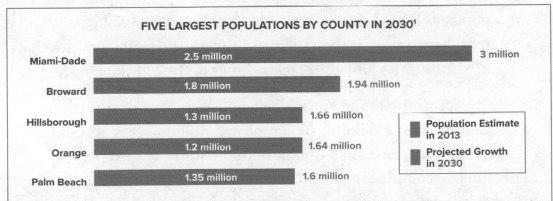

FIVE LARGEST POPULATIONS BY COUNTY IN 2030[1]

Miami-Dade: 2.5 million / 3 million
Broward: 1.8 million / 1.94 million
Hillsborough: 1.3 million / 1.66 million
Orange: 1.2 million / 1.64 million
Palm Beach: 1.35 million / 1.6 million

■ Population Estimate in 2013
■ Projected Growth in 2030

[1] Data from University of Florida's Bureau of Economic and Business Research (BEBR) Projections of Florida Population by County 2015-2040

FIND TEXT EVIDENCE

Paragraph 1
Read the highlighted claim in paragraph 1.

Paragraphs 2–4
Circle the words that tell why Deseret Ranch decided to develop its land.

Population Graph
Compare the population estimate with the projected growth estimate. What can you infer about Florida's high-population counties?

_____

_____

_____

_____

_____

_____

Take Notes Paraphrase the author's claim, and give examples of supporting details.

SOURCE 2

Fund Florida FOREVER!

5   Florida Forever is Florida's largest land protection program. It needs significantly more funding to protect areas of undeveloped natural lands. **If Florida Forever does not receive more funding, the program cannot protect thousands of acres of wilderness.** Without protection, these natural lands are turned into urban developments, which threaten humans, wildlife, and nature.

6   Urban development may help address Florida's growing population, but it destroys Florida's unique and vital ecosystems. The barrier islands in the Panhandle protect the mainland from storms. Ranchlands in Central Florida are sources of clean drinking water. South Florida's wetlands control floods. Above all, urbanization creates pollution, which is the primary cause of rising sea levels that threaten Florida's coastal communities.

7   Urban development also threatens Florida's biodiversity. Plants and animals depend on Florida's ecosystems to survive. Without biodiversity, animals can become extinct. Jim Strickland manages Blackbeard's Ranch. He believes it's an obligation and a privilege to protect the ranchland's wildlife. In fact, he says that urbanization is already a major threat to the Florida panther.

8   According to the Florida Fish and Wildlife Conservation Commission's Wildlife 2060 report, 7 million acres of natural lands could be turned into development in the next 50 years. We must accommodate Florida's population growth without urban development. Florida Forever must get more funding. Future generations of people, wildlife, and Florida itself depend on it.

ReVITALIZe
FLORIDA'S DOWNTOWNS

9   As Florida's population rapidly grows, elected officials, conservationists, and community organizers look for solutions. One way to meet Florida's population growth and preserve its natural areas is to revitalize downtown neighborhoods.

10   First, revitalizing downtown areas instills a sense of pride. Districts' historic homes, abandoned buildings, or empty lots can be turned into new homes and business opportunities. In Tampa, for example, the old federal courthouse sat vacant for fifteen years before it was converted to a hotel.

11   Second, revitalization creates a sense of community. Preserved open spaces and pedestrian-friendly streets invite people to stroll and gather. In 2018, the city of Coral Gables completed its Miracle Mile makeover. Now residents and visitors can enjoy its shops and restaurants.

12   Third, revitalization encourages growth. Combined with Florida's climate and recreational activities, it also enhances quality of life. For instance, the city of Fort Myers will redevelop its vacant riverfront district. It will add more than four thousand residential units, and create more parks and public spaces. Community organizers in Pensacola have also presented plans to revitalize its downtown districts.

13   Revitalization fosters a strong sense of place in these communities. It is also key to solving Florida's population crisis and protecting its natural lands. Let's invest in our downtowns.

FIND TEXT EVIDENCE 🔍

Paragraph 9
Underline the sentence that states the author's claim about meeting Florida's growing population.

Paragraphs 10–11
Draw a box around the claim about what revitalization will do. How did Coral Gables revitalize its downtown?

_____

_____

Paragraphs 12–13
Circle how many residential units Fort Myers will add downtown. What other city has plans to revitalize its downtown?

_____

_____

Take Notes Paraphrase the author's claim, and give examples of supporting details.

My Goal I can synthesize information from three sources.

TAKE NOTES

Read the writing prompt below. Write your claim. Then use the three sources, your notes, and the graphic organizer to plan a response.

Writing Prompt *Write an argumentative essay to present to your class. Answer the question: Should Florida's government use funds to protect natural lands or to develop land?*

Synthesize Information

Review the pros and cons of each source. What do you think is the best solution? What evidence convinced you? Discuss your ideas with a partner.

CHECK IN 〉 1 〉 2 〉 3 〉 4 〉

Plan: Organize Ideas

Claim	Reasons
Florida's government should use its funds to . . . It is a good idea / not a good idea that Florida's government should . . .	One reason that Florida's government should use its funds . . .

Relevant Evidence

Source 1	Source 2	Source 3

Draft: Relevant Evidence

Support Your Claim Once you form your claim, you will need to support it with logical reasons and relevant evidence from multiple reliable sources. Relevant evidence includes facts, examples, and important details that are connected to your topic. As you plan your first draft, look at the evidence in your writer's notebook and in your graphic organizer on page 95. After you review your evidence, ask yourself these questions:

- Does each piece of evidence support a reason for my claim?
- Did I copy all numbers and quotations correctly from my sources?
- Did I give strong evidence to persuade readers to believe my claim?
- How can I present my reasons and evidence in a logical way?

List two strong examples of relevant evidence you will use in your essay.

_____

_____

_____

Draft Use your graphic organizer and examples above to write your draft in your writer's notebook. Before you start writing, review the rubric on page 86. Remember to indent each paragraph and cite your sources.

Grammar Connections

When you find facts and details from sources, be sure to keep track of these sources. Here are examples of sentence starters that include information from sources:

- *According to this article, "Nature Is Important"...*
- *Research shows that ...*
- *As pointed out before in "Our National Parks" ...*
- *The article "Nature" ...*

CHECK IN ▶ 1 ⟩ 2 ⟩ 3 ⟩ 4

Revise: Peer Conferences

Review a Draft Listen actively to your partner. Take notes about what you liked and what was difficult to follow. Begin by telling what you liked. Use these sentence starters.

Your claim was persuasive because . . .
What did you mean by . . .
I think adding more facts can help to . . .

After you finish giving each other feedback, reflect on the peer conference. Which suggestion did you find to be the most helpful?

_____

_____

Revision Use the Revising Checklist to help you figure out what text you may need to move, elaborate on, or delete. After you finish writing your final draft, use the full rubric on pages 236–239 to score your essay.

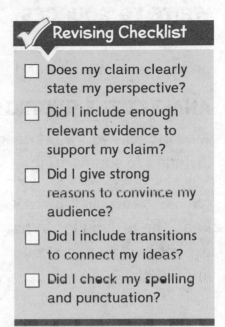

Next, you'll write an argumentative essay on a new topic.

✓ Revising Checklist

- ☐ Does my claim clearly state my perspective?
- ☐ Did I include enough relevant evidence to support my claim?
- ☐ Did I give strong reasons to convince my audience?
- ☐ Did I include transitions to connect my ideas?
- ☐ Did I check my spelling and punctuation?

My Score			
Purpose, Focus, & Organization (4 pts)	Evidence & Elaboration (4 pts)	Conventions (2 pts)	Total (10 pts)

WRITING

WRITE TO SOURCES

You will answer an argumentative prompt using sources and a rubric.

ANALYZE THE RUBRIC

A rubric tells you what needs to be included in your writing.

Purpose, Focus, and Organization

Read the fifth bullet. What do you expect to read in a strong introduction?

A strong introduction _____

_____

_____

Evidence and Elaboration

Read the second bullet. Why is it important to use more than one source?

_____

_____

_____

Evidence and Elaboration

Underline the word in the second bullet that tells you what kind of evidence supports the argument.

Argumentative Writing Rubric

Purpose, Focus, and Organization • Score 4

- stays focused on the purpose, audience, and task
- makes a claim that clearly supports a perspective
- uses transitional strategies, such as words and phrases, to connect ideas
- presents ideas in a logical progression, or order
- **begins with a strong introduction and ends with a strong conclusion**

Evidence and Elaboration • Score 4

- effectively supports the claim with logical reasons
- has strong examples of relevant evidence, or supporting details, from multiple sources
- uses elaborative techniques, such as examples, definitions, and quotations from sources
- expresses interesting ideas clearly using precise language
- uses appropriate academic and domain-specific language
- uses different sentence structures

Turn to page 236 for the complete Argumentative Writing Rubric.

Strong Introduction

Write an Effective Introduction Your introduction should explain the topic of your argumentative essay. It should also clearly state your claim in which you share your perspective, or attitude, about the topic. Read the paragraph below. The author's claim is highlighted.

Audience

Writers first consider their audience before they write. Knowing their audience helps writers decide how to grab their attention. An introduction with a question, an anecdote, a quotation, or an interesting fact that relates to your topic can get your audience to start thinking about the topic and support your argument.

> On a hot day in Apalachicola, Florida, in 1841, John Gorrie invented the ice-making machine to keep his patients cool as they suffered from fever. His ice machine would lead to the invention of the refrigerator and the air conditioner. It has been debated that Gorrie did not invent the air conditioner, but to many Floridians, he is still respected. In 2014, he was inducted into the Florida Inventors Hall of Fame. **Indeed, Gorrie should be considered a leading pioneer in cooling systems.**

What details in the introduction above immediately grab your attention?

_____

_____

_____

What does the author's claim tell you about his or her perspective?

_____

_____

_____

ANALYZE THE STUDENT MODEL

Paragraph 1

How does Rita get the reader's attention in her introduction?

_____

_____

_____

Read the first paragraph of Rita's essay. Her claim has been highlighted.

Paragraph 2

Draw a box around the words that explain how technology converts natural resources into energy. How does this evidence support Rita's perspective?

_____

_____

_____

Underline the sources that Rita uses to support her claim.

Student Model: Argumentative Essay

Rita responded to the Writing Prompt: _Write an argumentative essay to present to your class. Answer the question: Should we use natural sources for energy?_ Read Rita's essay below.

1   Why wouldn't we use Earth's natural resources to make energy? We use Earth's natural resources every day. The sun's rays help plants and animals grow. We go fishing in the oceans and rivers. The wind keeps us cool. We use these resources daily, so why not for energy? Even though using natural resources means harming some, these sources are unlimited, clean, and renewable. Therefore, we should use Earth's natural resources to make energy.

2   We get a lot of energy from natural resources. In fact, 75 percent of America's renewable energy comes from hydropower plants in rivers, according to the article "Hydropower, Our Leading Renewable Energy Source." We use technology to generate energy from these natural resources. The hydropower process in the diagram in the "Hydropower, Our Leading Renewable Energy Source" article shows exactly how we use dams, generators, and turbines to create energy from moving water. We use drills and turbines to produce energy from deep within Earth's crust, says the article "Geothermal Energy Is Available Energy." Geothermal energy can make fifty thousand times more energy than coal energy!

(bkgd) Titus Group/Shutterstock; (inset) Nata Studio/Shutterstock

3   However, some ecologists worry about the ecosystems the technologies harm. Fish get blocked by dams and cannot swim upriver to reproduce. Solar plants take up a lot of space in the desert where desert tortoises live. Toxic water from geothermal plants gets into rivers. Birds and bats crash into or get electrocuted by wind turbines, says the American Bird Conservancy.

4   So should we use these energy sources even if they harm living things? To many, renewable energy is still the right choice because it is the only choice. Renewable energy does not get used up at all. According to the article "Solar Energy: Hot or Not?" many ecologists approve of the idea of renewable energy. Some are trying to minimize the ecological impact of these new technologies. For example, fish ladders help fish swim upriver. The article "Wind Energy Threatens Wildlife" suggests building future wind farms far away from places where birds fly through.

5   Using technology to generate power from Earth's natural resources isn't perfect. Some ecosystems are harmed in the process. But Earth provides us with an endless supply of heat, water, wind, and sunshine. We should take advantage of these unlimited, clean, and renewable natural resources to generate energy in the future.

FatCamera/E+/Getty Images

ARGUMENTATIVE ESSAY

Paragraph 3

Rita presents an opposing argument in paragraph 3. **Draw a box** around the claim. **Underline** evidence that supports this claim.

Paragraph 4

Rita presents her counterargument to the opposing claim. Paraphrase her argument.

_____

_____

_____

Paragraph 5

Circle the words from Rita's conclusion that are repeated from her introduction. Why is this repetition important?

_____

_____

_____

Apply the Rubric

With a partner, use the rubric on page 98 to discuss why Rita scored a 4 on her essay.

Analyze the Prompt

My Goal

I can write an argumentative essay.

Writing Prompt

Write an argumentative essay to present to your class. Answer the question: Did inventions of the past have a positive or negative effect?

Purpose, Audience, and Task Reread the writing prompt. What is your purpose for writing? My purpose is to _____

_____

Who will your audience be? My audience will be _____

_____

What type of writing is the prompt asking for? _____

_____

Set a Purpose for Reading Sources You will read a passage set about whether past inventions have had a positive or negative effect. The fourth source in the passage set will be "Getting from Here to There" on pages 56–57 in the **Literature Anthology.** Asking questions about the passage set will help you figure out your purpose for reading. Before you read the passage set, write a question here.

_____

_____

_____

_____

Read the following passage set.

Honoring Black Women Inventors of the Past

1   In the late 1800s, three black women invented items that improved people's home lives. Their names were Judy W. Reed, Sarah E. Goode, and Miriam E. Benjamin. **Although their names might be unfamiliar, their inventions should not be overlooked.** These inventions were as advanced then as computers are today.

2   In 1884, Judy W. Reed patented a hand-operated machine for kneading and rolling dough. In 1885, Sarah E. Goode patented a bed that folded into a cabinet that could serve as a desk. In 1888, Miriam E. Benjamin won a patent for a chair with a signal button. (This invention is still widely used today. The US House of Representatives and airplanes adopted similar chair methods.) These three inventions made everyday life much more efficient, says historian Ruth Schwartz Cowan.

3   These three women inventors earned patents. But it is disappointing that many others will never be known. Some women didn't apply for patents because they couldn't afford an attorney. Others applied for patents but didn't disclose their race. They were afraid that they would make less money if people knew that an African American had developed the invention.

4   Cowan regrets that domestic inventions aren't usually recognized as technology. It's true. Many of us think of technology as virtual or wireless. But these inventions should be remembered and respected. They made domestic labor easier and faster. Black women inventors of the 1800s deserve our recognition.

ARGUMENTATIVE ESSAY

FIND TEXT EVIDENCE

Paragraphs 1–2

Circle the names of the three inventors. Read the highlighted claim in paragraph 1. How did these three inventions help people?

_____

_____

_____

_____

Paragraphs 3–4

What were some of the issues that black women inventors faced?

_____

_____

_____

_____

_____

Take Notes Paraphrase the author's claim, and give examples of supporting details.

WRITING

FIND TEXT EVIDENCE

Paragraph 5

Read the highlighted detail in the introduction. What does this detail tell you about the topic of the argumentative essay?

_____

_____

_____

Paragraphs 6–7

Underline the detail that tells you why telegraphs were forgotten.

Paragraphs 8–9

Why is Morse code useful to the US Navy today?

_____

_____

_____

_____

Take Notes Paraphrase the author's claim, and give examples of supporting details.

MORSE CODE
IS SAFE AND RELIABLE

5   In 1844, Samuel Morse sent the first successful telegraph message from Washington, D.C., to Baltimore. **He invented the nonwritten telegraph message system known as Morse code. He could not know then that his invention would still be used in the twenty-first century.** While only a small number of people use Morse code today, more people should learn this important communication tool. It is a guaranteed safe and reliable system.

6   In the 1800s, sending a telegraph was fast, but it wasn't easy. Trained operators needed to send accurate messages at top speed. Only one message at a time could cross the wires. Then telegraphs were forgotten after the telephone was invented.

7   However, Morse code itself was never obsolete. In 2017, the US Navy successfully tested a Morse code lamplight signal system to "text" ship to ship. When sailors on the USS *Stout* sent text messages, the system converted those texts to Morse code lamplight signals. Sailors on the USS *Monterey* received and interpreted these signals.

8   According to Scott Lowery, an engineer at the Naval Surface Warfare Center in Florida, the system is intuitive. It can't be jammed nor hacked. Most importantly, it can be used if the power or satellite communications get broken or lost. For those instances, says Office of Naval Research Command Master Chief Matt Matteson, the system is invaluable.

9   There is no doubt that using Morse code can keep us safe. More people should use this reliable communication system.

ALL ABOARD
ON AMERICA'S RAIL SYSTEM

10   One hundred and fifty years after the first transcontinental railroad was built, the US rail system is still the most important mode of transportation. It truly is a symbol of progress.

11   In the 1860s, cross-country travel was a daunting trip. When the idea of the transcontinental railroad was proposed, it was an unusual but exciting idea. Workers raced to complete laying the tracks. Many were injured or killed during accidents, storms, or raids. Chinese workers set explosives to break through mountain rock. This was a dangerous task. The permanent rails also changed life for the roaming Plains Native Americans. They were forced to live on reservations by the US government.

12   Despite these deaths and displacements, the railroad was finally done by 1869. Now the country was united from coast to coast. Cross-country travel was affordable and efficient! Before 1869, New York travelers spent several months and over $1,000 to go to California by wagon. After 1869, the San Francisco to Omaha trip took a week and cost $83.25 for a one-way first-class ticket.

13   Similarly, the rail system today is focusing on efficiency. The US High Speed Rail Association wants a high-speed rail system in place by 2030. This system will significantly reduce congestion, traffic, and pollution once completed.

14   America's rail system has faced problems over time, but these problems result from improvements for better service. Its priority has always been and continues to be providing affordable and efficient service. That's why it is a symbol of progress.

ARGUMENTATIVE ESSAY

FIND TEXT EVIDENCE

Paragraph 10

Reread the introduction. **Circle** the author's claim.

Paragraph 11

Underline the dangers to the Chinese workers. How did the railroad impact the lives of the Plains Native Americans?

_____

_____

_____

Paragraphs 12–14

How did the railroad improve people's lives? How does it continue to help people?

_____

_____

_____

_____

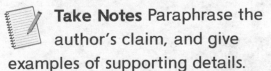 **Take Notes** Paraphrase the author's claim, and give examples of supporting details.

My Goal I can synthesize information from four sources.

TAKE NOTES

Read the writing prompt below. Write your claim. Then use the four sources, your notes, and the graphic organizer to plan a response.

Writing Prompt *Write an argumentative essay to present to your class. Answer the question: Did inventions of the past have a positive or negative effect?*

Synthesize Information

Review the evidence recorded from each source. How does the information show how inventions of the past were positive or negative? Discuss your ideas with a partner.

CHECK IN   1   2   3   4

Plan: Organize Ideas

Claim	Reasons
Inventions of the past were . . . These inventions were a good idea/not a good idea because . . .	One reason that inventions of the past were . . .

Relevant Evidence

Source 1	Source 2	Source 3	Source 4

Draft: Elaboration

Include Elaborative Details When making an argument, strong writers use elaboration, or use details to develop his or her reasons. Elaboration includes relevant examples, facts, definitions, or quotations from sources.

After you decide on the reasons and elaborative details you will use, paraphrase this information. Paraphrasing means using your own words to restate details. Avoid plagiarism by keeping track of your sources so that you can cite them properly in your essay.

> Ecologists also worry about the height of the wind towers. In an article in *Scientific American*, ecologist Erin Baerwald says, "As turbine height increases, bat deaths increase exponentially." According to an official study presented in *Current Biology*, 90 percent of the bats die in a more grisly way other than collisions. The change in air pressure created by the rapidly spinning blades causes internal bleeding in bat lungs.

Read the example above from "Wind Energy Threatens Wildlife." Then paraphrase this information.

_____

_____

_____

 Draft Use your graphic organizer and the information above to write your draft in your writer's notebook. Before you start writing, review the rubric on page 98. Remember to indent each paragraph.

Grammar Connections

Remember to use italics or underlining with the title of a long work, such as a book or newspaper: *The Tallahassee Daily Times.* Use quotation marks with articles in journals or magazines: "Henry Flagler and Florida's Railway." Use quotation marks around a part of a book: *The name of the third chapter is "The Final Scene."*

CHECK IN 1 2 3 4

Revise: Peer Conferences

Review a Draft Listen actively to your partner. Take notes about what you liked and what was difficult to follow. Begin by telling what you liked. Use these sentence starters.

Your introduction grabbed my attention because . . .
Can you clarify what you meant . . .
I think adding another source can help to . . .

After you finish giving each other feedback, reflect on the peer conference. Which suggestion did you find to be the most helpful?

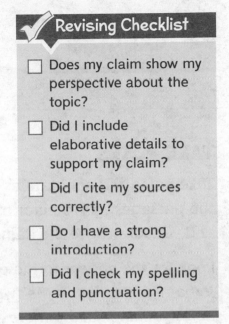

✓ **Revising Checklist**

☐ Does my claim show my perspective about the topic?

☐ Did I include elaborative details to support my claim?

☐ Did I cite my sources correctly?

☐ Do I have a strong introduction?

☐ Did I check my spelling and punctuation?

Revision Use the Revising Checklist to help you figure out what text you may need to move, elaborate on, or delete. After you finish writing your final draft, use the full rubric on pages 236–239 to score your essay.

Turn to page 85. Fill in the bars to show what you learned.

My Score			
Purpose, Focus, & Organization (4 pts)	Evidence & Elaboration (4 pts)	Conventions (2 pts)	Total (10 pts)

My Goal I can read and understand science texts.

TAKE NOTES

Take notes and annotate as you read the passages "A Protector of Nature" and "Children Save the Rain Forest."

Look for the answer to the question: *What information in the two texts helps you understand more about how human activities impact the environment?*

_____

_____

_____

_____

_____

_____

_____

PASSAGE 1

NARRATIVE NONFICTION

A Protector of NATURE

Many people have worked throughout the years to protect our country's natural lands. One such person was Margaret "Mardy" Thomas Murie. Murie's family had moved to Alaska when she was a young child. Her early years in Alaska gave her a love of nature that continued throughout her life.

From Alaska to Wyoming

While in college, Murie met Olaus Murie. He was a scientist studying caribou, a kind of deer. In 1924, Murie became the first woman to graduate from the University of Alaska. Soon, she and Olaus married. In 1927, Olaus was asked to study elk, another type of deer, in Wyoming. Murie assisted in his work and raised their children. While in Wyoming, they also began working with the Wilderness Society. This group worked with the government to save natural lands in Alaska. The Muries' work with the group led to the establishment of the Arctic National Wildlife Refuge in Alaska. The refuge would protect the environment and its diverse ecosystems and wildlife habitats. Today, the refuge has expanded to 19 million acres. The Muries also worked to pass the Wilderness Act. This act set up a government process to save natural areas.

Author and Speaker

After Olaus died in 1963, Murie continued their work. She went on to become an author, speaker, and public supporter of issues related to protecting natural areas. In 1968, she sold her Wyoming ranch, which

Bill Wunsch/The Denver Post/Getty Images

became part of the Grand Teton National Park. Murie stayed on to found and teach at the Teton Science School. In 1975, she wrote a report that recommended the protection of Alaskan lands. In 1980, Congress agreed to protect millions of acres of land in Alaska.

Murie won many honors for her work. She won the Presidential Medal of Freedom in 1998. This is the highest award that a person not in the military can receive in the United States. She died in Wyoming in 2003 at age 101. She is now known to many as the "grandmother" of the movement to protect nature.

PASSAGE 2 EXPOSITORY TEXT

CHILDREN SAVE THE RAIN FOREST

In 1987, first- and second-grade students in Sweden were so persistent about protecting the rain forest that they raised money to buy one!

Their teacher taught them about rain forests. They learned about howler monkeys, colorful birds, and poisonous frogs and snakes that lived there. They also learned that trees were cut down to create land for cattle grazing and farming. When they saw images of bulldozers cutting down these trees, they were horrified. They desperately wanted to help save the rain forests.

Then they met biologist Sharon Kinsman. She told them about rain forest land in Monteverde, Costa Rica, that could be purchased through the Monteverde Conservation League (MCL). The children decided to raise money to buy land. They worked tirelessly, from writing

TAKE NOTES

and performing songs to holding bake sales and even a fair! They raised over $2,000, enough to buy over one hundred acres of rain forest.

Soon, children from other schools joined the effort. The Swedish government gave a grant to buy land. The MCL decided to honor the children by naming the preserve Bosque Eterno de los Niños (BEN), or Children's Eternal Rainforest. The movement grew beyond Sweden. Eventually, children from forty-four countries helped raise $2 million.

Today, BEN protects more than 56,000 acres of rain forest. It is the largest private reserve in Costa Rica.

Costa Rica now serves as a model for reversing rain forest loss and protecting its biodiversity. Preserving the rain forest has worldwide benefits, such as protecting the water supply. Its trees take in vast quantities of carbon dioxide that help to reduce global warming. Its plants provide natural remedies for diseases.

Lindsay Stallcup, executive director of MCL, explains that Costa Rica had lost half of its forest cover between 1940 and 1987. But because of conservation efforts, much of the forest in Costa Rica is now protected. According to research in 2012, Costa Rica increased forest cover to 52 percent in 2010. It was all thanks to the Swedish schoolchildren who started the worldwide effort.

COMPARE THE PASSAGES

Review your notes from "A Protector of Nature" and "Children Save the
Rain Forest." Use your notes and the Venn diagram below to record how
information in the two passages is alike and different.

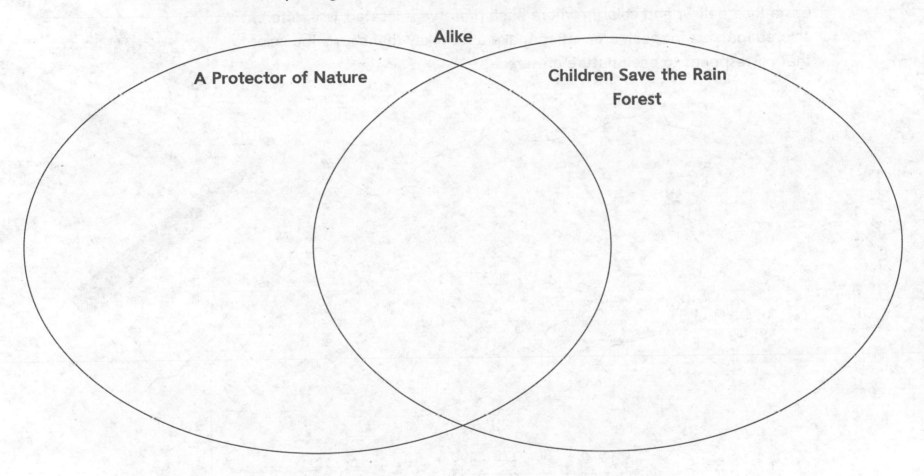

Alike

A Protector of Nature

Children Save the Rain
Forest

Synthesize Information

Think about both texts. Why is it important to protect the
environment? Write your response in your reader's notebook.

COMPLETE A MAP

Research facts about the Arenal Volcano National Park, the Children's Eternal Rainforest, the Alberto Manuel Brenes Biological Reserve, and the Monteverde Cloud Forest Preserve in Costa Rica. Use the map outline of Costa Rica below, and color in where each preserve is located. Use different colored markers for each area. Then make a map key that shows the color that corresponds to each nature preserve.

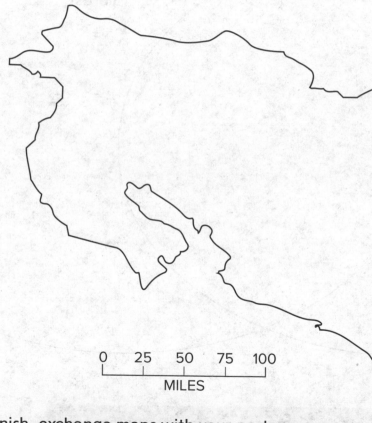

| 0 | 25 | 50 | 75 | 100 |

MILES

After you finish, exchange maps with your partner and discuss any other questions you have.

WRITE AN ESSAY

Use your completed map, your research notes, and information from the passages to write an essay. Answer this question: How does protecting the rain forest benefit Costa Rica?

_____

_____

_____

_____

_____

_____

_____

_____

_____

_____

_____

_____

_____

My Goal I can read and understand social studies texts.

TAKE NOTES

Take notes and annotate as you read the passages "The NYC Subway: An Interview with a Transit Supervisor" and "Solutions, Not Complaints."

Look for the answer to the question: *What information helps you understand why transportation systems are constantly being improved?*

_____
_____
_____
_____
_____
_____
_____
_____

PASSAGE 1

INTERVIEW

THE NYC SUBWAY

An Interview with a Transit Supervisor

Joseph Leader is a former chief maintenance officer at NYC Transit. He hasn't worked in New York for some years now, but he is proud of his tenure at NYC Transit. He enjoyed providing a service that has become an integral mode of transportation in New York City since the early 1900s.

Question: Can you describe a problem that affected ridership?

Answer: One tunnel is a major subway artery between Queens and Manhattan. It was built in the early 1900s for electric trolleys. A few years ago, it experienced a problem with its track circuits. It was caused by the tunnel's old age and too much water flooding it.

For the signals to work, a train on the track must proceed before another train behind it can move. In this tunnel, the signal stayed red instead of changing, so service was messed up. When it failed, it forced emergency crews to take the track out of service. We had to figure out a quick short-term fix because one of the busiest train lines uses this tunnel.

Question: How did you handle it?

Answer: It was difficult to fix because the tunnel is narrow. It's too dangerous to have men working there while trains are running. We stopped service so we could do emergency work. The crew replaced old steel plates, rewired the entire track circuit, and replaced track rails. Finally, they tested all signal circuits to ensure that everything was working properly. We did a lot of work in a little amount of time because we wanted to restore service quickly.

Question: Parts of the subway system are more than one hundred years old. Are there some repairs or issues that need constant attention?

Answer: The system is holding up well. But NYC Transit works at it. Everything wears out, from the rails, the wheels, the cars. They wear out at different times and for different reasons. That's why NYC Transit has a maintenance program. It makes sure that the system works.

 PASSAGE 2

PERSONAL NARRATIVE

Solutions, Not COMPLAINTS

Every day, Mom and I leave our house early in the morning. We live outside the city, but my school is located downtown. To get to and from school every day, I change from one city bus to another halfway through the ride.

One day, I had had enough. I was weary and frustrated. "I wish that the light rail train stopped in our neighborhood! Our trip would be so much easier!" I cried out. It can be so difficult to get around with my wheelchair.

"Maybe you should take that up with the mayor," Mom suggested. She always encouraged solutions over complaints.

Later that night, I took Mom's advice. I wrote a letter to the mayor.

TAKE NOTES

_____

_____

_____

_____

_____

_____

_____

_____

_____

_____

_____

_____

_____

_____

_____

_____

_____

_____

Dear Mr. Mayor,

My name is Sofia Martinez. Every day, I take two city buses to and from school. I change buses halfway through my trip because there is no direct route from my house to school, which is located downtown. This means that my mom and I miss out on sleep and time with our family in the mornings. Also, I'm not the only person in my neighborhood who faces this problem. My neighbor works at the city hospital. He takes two buses to and from work every day, too.

I have a solution to this problem. The light rail train route should be extended to include a stop in my neighborhood.

I know that this solution will cost money. But I think the cost is worth it. The train will decrease the traffic and pollution. Some people drive cars because they don't want the hassle of changing buses. If they could take the train directly to work, they might leave their cars at home. Finally, the train is easy to get on and off, and the cost to ride is low.

Thank you for taking the time to read my letter. Please think about my idea.

Sincerely, Sofia Martinez

COMPARE THE PASSAGES

Review your notes from "The NYC Subway: An Interview with a Transit Supervisor" and "Solutions, Not Complaints." Use the Venn diagram below to record how the information in the two passages is alike and different.

Alike

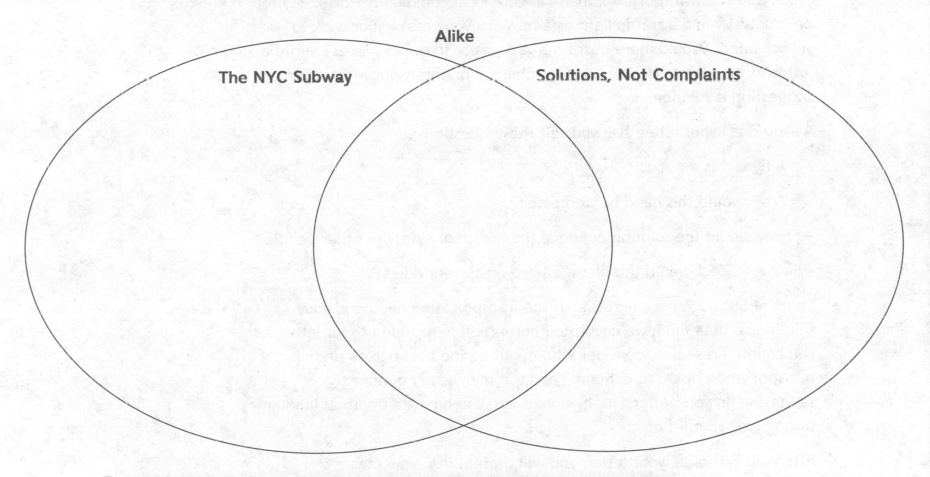

The NYC Subway

Solutions, Not Complaints

Synthesize Information

Think about both texts. How can new technology advance current or old transportation systems? Write your ideas in your reader's notebook.

CONNECT TO CONTENT

WRITE A LETTER

Wherever you live, people rely on transportation to get them around safely and efficiently.

Think about a transportation need in your local community, town, city, or county. Would a traffic light or a new sidewalk make your walk to school safer? Would more buses make it easier to get to places? Write a letter to the transportation board explaining one transportation need and suggesting a solution.

As you draft your letter, ask yourself these questions:

• Why is this a need?

• Why should this need be addressed?

• How would the solution enhance the health or safety of other people?

• What effect would this change have on current riders?

Think about how you will research the transportation need and your solution so that you have accurate information to include in your letter. As you conduct research, consider who might be the best person on the transportation board to contact. Then use the correct greeting, or salutation, in your letter. Finally, make sure you have used formal language throughout your letter.

After you complete your letter, you will present it to your class.

Reflect on Your Learning

Talk About It Reflect on what you learned in this unit. Then talk with a partner about how you did.

I am really proud of how I can _____

_____

_____

_____

Something I need to work on more is _____

_____

_____

_____

My Goal Set a goal for Unit 2. In your reader's notebook, write about what you can do to get there.

Share a goal you have with a partner.

Build Knowledge

Essential Question

What do good problem solvers do?

Build Vocabulary

Write new words you learned about how people solved problems during colonial times. Draw lines and circles for the words you write.

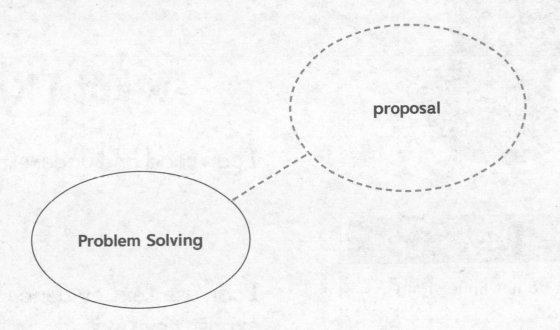

proposal

Problem Solving

Go online to **my.mheducation.com** and read the "Meet Me in the Middle" Blast. Think about how you feel when you have to compromise. Why is learning to compromise important? Then blast back your response.

Think about what you already know. Wherever you are is okay. Fill in the bars.

What I Know Now

I can read and understand expository text.

1 2 3 4

I can use text evidence to respond to expository text.

1 2 3 4

I know what good problem solvers do.

1 2 3 4

Key	
1 =	I do not understand.
2 =	I understand but need more practice.
3 =	I understand.
4 =	I understand and can teach someone.

STOP You will come back to the next page later.

Think about what you learned. Fill in the bars. Keep doing your best!

What I Learned

I can read and understand expository text.

1 > 2 > 3 > 4

I can use text evidence to respond to expository text.

1 > 2 > 3 > 4

I know what good problem solvers do.

1 > 2 > 3 > 4

My Goal I can read and understand expository text.

TAKE NOTES

As you read, make note of interesting words and important information.

_____

_____

_____

_____

_____

_____

_____

_____

_____

_____

_____

_____

_____

_____

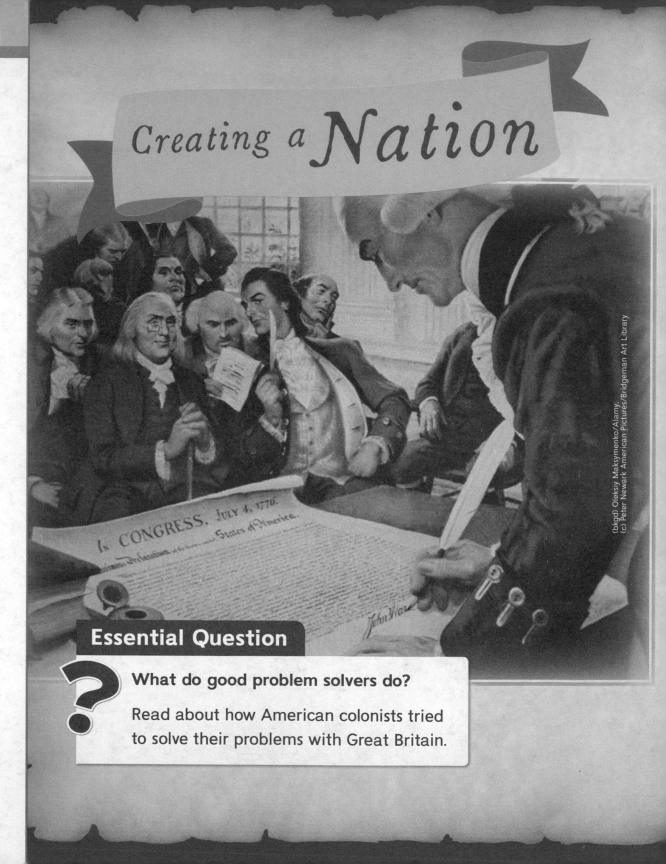

Creating a Nation

Essential Question

?

What do good problem solvers do?

Read about how American colonists tried to solve their problems with Great Britain.

Taxes and Protests

In 1765, King George III of Great Britain needed money to rule his empire. How could he raise it? With taxes! Parliament, the law-making branch of the British government, passed a new tax called the Stamp Act. Every piece of paper sold in the American colonies had to carry a special stamp. Want to buy a newspaper? Stamp! Pay the tax.

To most colonists, the Stamp Act was unfair. The citizens of Great Britain had the right to choose **representatives** to speak for them in Parliament. Although British citizens, the colonists had no such right. How could Parliament tax them if they had no voice in government?

The colonists held protests against the Stamp Act. Consequently, it was repealed, or canceled. But more taxes followed. Women protested a tax on cloth imported from Britain. How? They wove their own cloth at home.

Boston Tea Party: Colonists throw tea into the harbor.

Before long, the **situation** grew worse. In 1770, British soldiers fired into a disorderly crowd in Boston. Five colonists died. This tragedy is known as the Boston Massacre.

By 1773, most taxes had been repealed, or canceled, except the one on tea. One night, colonists held a protest called the Boston Tea Party. Dressed in disguise, they slipped onto three British ships in Boston Harbor and then they tossed the ships' cargo—tea—overboard.

Anonymous/Getty Images

FIND TEXT EVIDENCE

Read

Paragraphs 1-2

Problem and Solution

Underline the problem King George III faced. Write it here.

_____

_____

Circle the king's solution to the problem. Discuss why the colonists thought the Stamp Act was unfair.

_____

_____

Paragraphs 3-5

Reread

Draw a box around text evidence that tells how the colonists reacted to taxes imposed by the British.

Reread

Author's Craft

How does the author use text structure to demonstrate the relationship between the British and the colonists?

FIND TEXT EVIDENCE

Read

▼

Paragraphs 1-2

Problem and Solution

Circle the ways in which colonists differed on how to solve and resolve problems with the king. Based on this information, what inference can you make about the mood in the colonies at that time?

_____

_____

_____

_____

Paragraphs 3-5

Reread

Underline the names of the two people appointed by Congress to help with the conflict.

Reread

Author's Craft

Why is "Revolution Begins" a good heading for this section?

Revolution Begins

An angry King George punished the colonies by ordering the port of Boston closed and town meetings banned. Colonists called these harsh actions the "Intolerable Acts." However, they could not agree on how to **resolve** the problems with Great Britain. Patriots wanted to fight for independence. Loyalists wanted peace with the king. Many colonists were undecided.

Finally, colonists called for representatives from each colony to attend a **convention**. This important meeting, the First Continental Congress, took place in 1774 in Philadelphia. After discussion, the delegates decided to send a peace **proposal** to the king. Congress ended, but the trouble continued. In April 1775, there were rumors that the British were marching to Lexington and Concord, villages near Boston, to capture weapons that the patriots had hidden there.

The colonial militias were ready. Militias were groups of volunteers willing to fight. British troops attacked. The militias fired back. Surprisingly, the British retreated, or went back.

Now that war had begun, the patriots called for a Second Continental Congress in May. Delegates made George Washington commander of the new Continental Army. Congress also sent another peace proposal to King George.

As war continued, Congress formed **committees** to do important tasks. Five delegates were chosen to write a declaration of independence. This committee gave the job to one of its members—Thomas Jefferson.

Oleksiy Maksymenko/Alamy

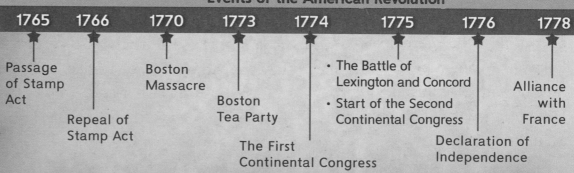

Events of the American Revolution

1765	1766	1770	1773	1774	1775	1776	1778

Passage of Stamp Act

Repeal of Stamp Act

Boston Massacre

Boston Tea Party

The First Continental Congress

• The Battle of Lexington and Concord
• Start of the Second Continental Congress

Declaration of Independence

Alliance with France

Independence Declared

Jefferson knew he had to convince many colonists of the need for independence. As a result, he combined a variety of ideas to make his case. Individuals, he explained, had certain rights. These included life, liberty, and the pursuit of happiness. Governments were created to protect those rights. Instead, King George had taken away colonists' rights and freedoms. Therefore, the colonies had to separate from Britain.

Congress went on to **debate** Jefferson's points. As a result, his strong words against slavery were deleted. There were other compromises, too. But on July 4, 1776, Congress approved the Declaration of Independence. A nation was born. Washington's army fought on. Finally, in 1778, France joined the fight on America's side.

This was a turning point. In 1781, British troops surrendered in the war's last major battle. That year, Congress approved the Articles of Confederation. This document outlined a government for the former colonies. The United States was created as a confederation, or a **union**, of separate states. The Articles gave the states, rather than a central government, the power to make most decisions.

In 1783, King George finally recognized the nation's independence. By then, though, the United States government clearly wasn't working very well. The states often didn't agree with one another.

The revolution had ended. The work of shaping a government had just started. It would continue with a Constitutional Convention in 1787.

1781
- Last major battle of the war
- Approval of the Articles of Confederation

1783
King George recognizes independence of United States

Summarize

Use your notes and the timeline to orally summarize important events and details in "Creating a Nation."

FIND TEXT EVIDENCE

Read

Paragraphs 1–5
Context Clues

Circle context clues that help you determine the meaning of *liberty*.

Timeline

Look at the timeline. Did the Boston Tea Party take place before the repeal of the Stamp Act or after?

_____

_____

_____

_____

_____

Reread

Author's Craft

What do you think was the most important characteristic needed among the men responsible for creating the Declaration of Independence? Explain your answer.

Vocabulary

Use the example sentences to talk with a partner about each word. Then answer the questions.

committees

I am on one of the **committees** to plan our winter class trip.

What committees could help to plan a school talent show?

_____

_____

convention

We learned the difference between bugs and insects at the science **convention**.

What are two words that mean the same as _convention_?

_____

_____

debate

My classmates like to **debate**, or discuss their different opinions.

What words help you know what _debate_ means?

_____

_____

proposal

The mayor shared a new **proposal** to build a library.

What proposal can you make to raise money for the field trip?

_____

_____

representatives

Our government **representatives** help to make and pass laws.

Who is the fifth-grade representative on the student council?

_____

_____

 Build Your Word List Reread the first paragraph on page 128. Circle the word _Patriots_. In your reader's notebook, use a word web to write more forms of the word. For example, write _patriotic_. Use a dictionary to help you find more related words.

resolve

To **resolve** the argument over our food choices, Ms. Smith asked Joe to look up facts on nutrition.

Who helps you to resolve a problem?

_____

_____

situation

The icy roads caused a dangerous driving **situation**.

What kind of weather can cause a serious flooding situation?

_____

_____

union

The United States is a **union** of 50 states that joined together.

What two U.S. states are not physically joined to the rest of the union?

_____

_____

Context Clues

Writers may define or restate the meaning of a difficult word by using commas and the clue word *or*. At other times, they may define the word in a nearby sentence.

🔍 FIND TEXT EVIDENCE

I'm not sure what repealed *means in the sentence* "By 1773 most taxes had been repealed, or canceled, except the one on tea." *But I see from the comma and the words* or canceled *that* repealed *means "canceled."*

By 1773 most taxes had been repealed, or canceled, except the one on tea.

Your Turn Use context clues to figure out the meanings of the following words in "Creating a Nation."

Parliament, page 127 _____

_____

retreated, page 128 _____

CHECK IN ▷ 1 ⟩ 2 ⟩ 3 ⟩ 4 ⟩

Anonymous/Getty Images

Reread

As you read, you should monitor, or check, your comprehension to make sure you understand the meaning of the text. When you read something that confuses you, you may have to go back and reread an earlier part of the selection. Rereading can help you check your understanding of facts and details in "Creating a Nation."

 FIND TEXT EVIDENCE

When you read the second paragraph of the section "Revolution Begins" on page 128, you may be confused about why the British troops began marching to Lexington and Concord.

Page 128

After discussion, the delegates decided to send a peace **proposal** to the king. Congress ended, but the trouble continued.

When I reread <u>the delegates decided to send a peace proposal to the king. Congress ended, but the trouble continued</u>, *I ask myself, "Why did the trouble continue even though the delegates sent a peace plan?" I can make the inference that King George did not agree to the proposal.*

 Your Turn Reread page 128. Discuss and retell how the patriots responded to the British troops marching to Lexington and Concord. What happened after the British troops attacked? Reread to find the answer.

_____

_____

_____

CHECK IN 1 2 3 4

Headings and Timelines

The selection "Creating a Nation" is expository text. Expository text gives facts, examples, and explanations about a topic. It may include text features such as headings, charts, diagrams, or timelines that organize information.

FIND TEXT EVIDENCE

I can tell that "Creating a Nation" is expository text because it gives facts about events that led up to and followed the American Revolution. I also see headings and a timeline.

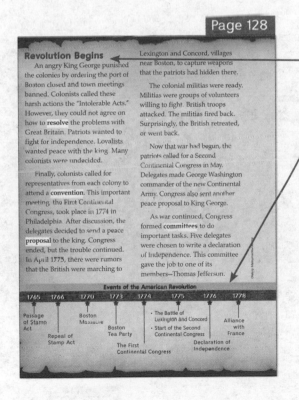

Page 128

Revolution Begins

An angry King George punished the colonies by ordering the port of Boston closed and town meetings banned. Colonists called these harsh actions the "Intolerable Acts." However, they could not agree on how to **resolve** the problems with Great Britain. Patriots wanted to fight for independence. Loyalists wanted peace with the king. Many colonists were undecided.

Finally, colonists called for representatives from each colony to attend a **convention**. This important meeting, the First Continental Congress, took place in 1774 in Philadelphia. After discussion, the delegates decided to send a peace **proposal** to the king. Congress ended, but the trouble continued. In April 1775, there were rumors that the British were marching to

Lexington and Concord, villages near Boston, to capture weapons that the patriots had hidden there.

The colonial militias were ready. Militias were groups of volunteers willing to fight. British troops attacked. The militias fired back. Surprisingly, the British retreated, or went back.

Now that war had begun, the patriots called for a Second Continental Congress in May. Delegates made George Washington commander of the new Continental Army. Congress also sent another peace proposal to King George.

As war continued, Congress formed **committees** to do important tasks. Five delegates were chosen to write a declaration of independence. This committee gave the job to one of its members—Thomas Jefferson.

Events of the American Revolution

1765	1766	1770	1773	1774	1775	1776	1778

Passage of Stamp Act

Repeal of Stamp Act

Boston Massacre

Boston Tea Party

The First Continental Congress

• The Battle of Lexington and Concord
• Start of the Second Continental Congress

Declaration of Independence

Alliance with France

Headings

A heading tells what a section of text is mostly about.

Timeline

A timeline is a diagram that shows events in the order they took place.

Your Turn Review and discuss the events on the timeline. Why did the author include the timeline? How is the information helpful?

COLLABORATE

CHECK IN 1 2 3 4

Problem and Solution

When an author uses a **problem and solution** text structure, the author presents a problem and then shares the solution, or the steps taken to solve it. Signal words can help you identify a problem (*question, problem, issue*) and a solution (*resolution, resolve, a consequence of, as a result,* and *so*).

🔍 FIND TEXT EVIDENCE

On page 129, I read that Jefferson's problem was to convince undecided colonists of the need for independence. The signal words as a result *tell me Jefferson's solution:* He combined many ideas to make his case for independence.

Problem	Solution
Some colonists didn't want independence.	Jefferson combined ideas to convince them.

Peter Newark American Pictures/Bridgeman Art Library

Your Turn Reread "Creating a Nation." Find other problems faced by the colonists and list them in your graphic organizer on page 135. Then identify how the colonists solved the problems.

CHECK IN 1 2 3 4

Problem	Solution

Respond to Reading

Discuss the prompt below. Use your notes and text evidence to support your ideas. Make sure to write a response that is a paragraph long.

Explain why the division between the colonists on whether or not to support the king was significant.

_____

_____

_____

_____

_____

_____

_____

_____

_____

_____

_____

_____

_____

Quick Tip

Use these sentence starters to discuss the text and to put your text evidence in order.

• *At first, the colonists . . .*

• *Then I read that . . .*

• *Finally, the colonists . . .*

Grammar Connections

Make sure that you have capitalized the names of people and the initials that stand for their names.

John Quincy Adams

J. Q. Adams

Remember that titles or abbreviations of titles, whether they come before or after the names of people, are capitalized.

Mr. Jefferson

King George III

CHECK IN ⟩ 1 ⟩ 2 ⟩ 3 ⟩ 4 ⟩

Founders Solve Problems

COLLABORATE

Many delegates worked together to solve issues. Their work led them to create a new system of government called the U. S. Constitution. Create a multimedia slideshow about the U. S. Constitution. Work collaboratively with a larger group.

Step 1 **Set a Goal** As part of your research, focus on the delegates who solved issues to create the U. S. Constitution. Include answers to questions such as: What is the U. S. Constitution? Why was it written? What is significant about how the delegates settled issues?

Step 2 **Identify Sources** Use online and print sources to find information about these delegates. These can be primary and secondary sources. Primary sources are original documents or accounts by people who took part in an event. Secondary sources are created by people who do not have firsthand knowledge of the topic.

Step 3 **Find and Record Information** Take notes. How does the information you found in a firsthand source compare with the information you found in a secondhand account of the same event? How do they differ? Cite your sources.

Step 4 **Organize and Synthesize Information** Organize your notes. Discuss the primary and secondary sources you find most helpful.

Step 5 **Create and Present** Create your multimedia slideshow. Your illustrations, photos, or music should emphasize or clarify your ideas. After you finish, you will share your work with the class.

Quick Tip

Examples of primary sources include delegates' letters, diary or journal entries, autobiographies, speeches, or historical documents. These examples give firsthand accounts about the Constitutional Convention or the Constitution.

Examples of secondary sources include textbooks and encyclopedias.

The image above shows a part of the Declaration of Independence.

CHECK IN 1 2 3 4

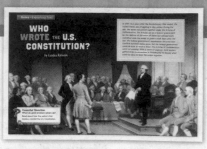

Who Wrote the U.S. Constitution?

? **What effect does the idiom *chewed over* create?**

Talk About It Reread **Literature Anthology** page 102. Discuss what the idiom means.

Cite Text Evidence Which words and phrases help you determine what effect the idiom creates? Write text evidence in the chart.

Text Evidence	What Effect It Creates

Write The idiom *chewed over* shows that _____

_____

_____

Literature Anthology: pages 96–111

Make Inferences

An idiom is an expression that has a figurative, or not literal, meaning. For example, the idiom *chewed over* does not mean that the delegates are chewing food. Use what you know about the delegates' feelings and thoughts to help you infer what the idiom means.

CHECK IN 1 2 3 4

How does the author build suspense in "The Great Compromise"?

COLLABORATE

Talk About It Reread **Literature Anthology** pages 104–105. Discuss how the author describes what happened on July 2, 1787.

Cite Text Evidence Which words and phrases does the author use to create suspense? Write text evidence in the chart.

Text Evidence	How It Builds Suspense

Write The author builds suspense by _____

_____

_____

 Quick Tip

Think about the events of July 2, 1787. Why are the states tied? How does this create suspense?

Synthesize Information

Combine what you already know about language with what you find in the text to create a new understanding. Think about what words signal suspense. Consider why the author chose to use those words in a social studies text.

CHECK IN 1 2 3 4

? How does the author use an anecdote to help you understand how Benjamin Franklin's outlook changes?

COLLABORATE

Talk About It Reread the last two paragraphs on page 110 of the **Literature Anthology**. Discuss what Franklin thought about the carving on Washington's chair.

Cite Text Evidence How does what Franklin thinks about the carving indicate that his outlook changed? Use text evidence to explain.

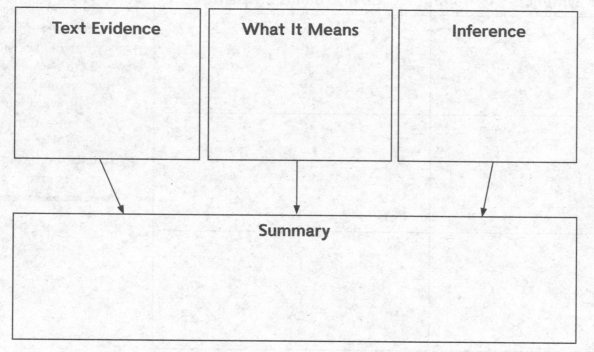

Text Evidence	What It Means	Inference

Summary

Write The anecdote helps me understand how Benjamin Franklin's outlook has changed by showing _____

_____

_____

CHECK IN ⟩ 1 ⟩ 2 ⟩ 3 ⟩ 4 ⟩

Respond to Reading

Discuss the prompt below. Use your notes and text evidence to support your response.

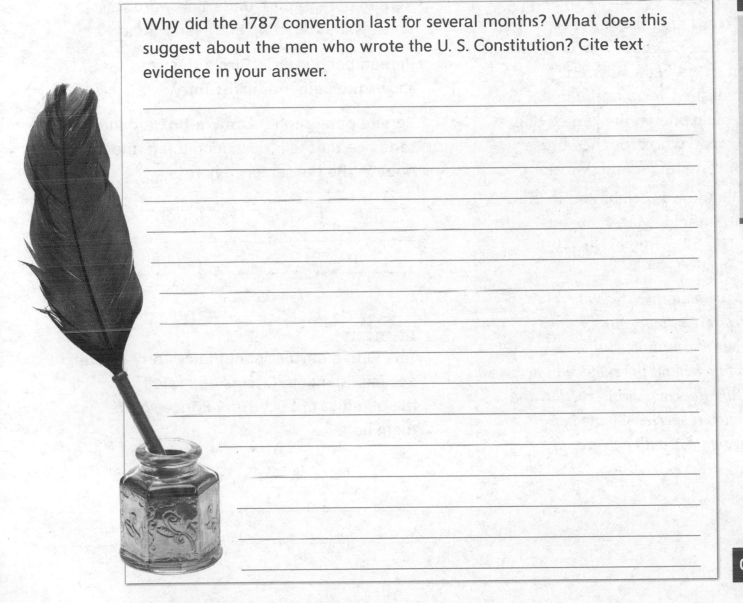

Why did the 1787 convention last for several months? What does this suggest about the men who wrote the U. S. Constitution? Cite text evidence in your answer.

_____

_____

_____

_____

_____

_____

_____

_____

_____

_____

_____

_____

CHECK IN 1 2 3 4

Yulia Reznikov/Alamy

Wordsmiths

Literature Anthology:
pages 114–117

1   Terry regularly used her voice to resolve problems and fight for social equality. When white neighbors attempted to claim the Princes' land as their own, they took their neighbors to court to address the situation. "Bars Fight," her only surviving poem, established Terry as the first African American female poet in the United States. Remembered as a woman who brought words to life, Terry died in 1821 in Sunderland, Vermont.

2   Terry's remarkable life was celebrated in *The Franklin Herald* of Greenfield, Massachusetts, with a lengthy obituary. The following excerpt was reprinted in *The Vermont Gazette*.

3   *In this remarkable woman there was an assemblage of qualities rarely to be found... Her volubility [ability to speak continuously] was exceeded by none, and in general the fluency of her speech was not destitute [lacking] of instruction and education. She was much respected among her acquaintance, who treated her with a degree of deference.*

Reread paragraph 1. **Underline** words and phrases that describe Lucy Terry Prince.

Reread paragraph 2. **Circle** the word that shows the author admires Terry.

Reread paragraph 3. **Draw a box** around the sentence that tells how people felt about the poet. Write the sentence here:

_____

_____

_____

COLLABORATE

Talk with a partner about Lucy Terry Prince's accomplishments. Discuss and retell the qualities of Lucy Terry Prince. Write them here:

_____

_____

_____

1   Wheatley is remembered as the first African American to publish a collection of poetry. She also wrote and sent a poem to General George Washington in 1775 that praised him for his success during the American Revolution. His response to her shows how highly regarded Wheatley was. Below is part of Washington's letter.

2   Mrs Phillis,

    I thank you most sincerely for your polite notice of me, in the elegant Lines you enclosed; and however undeserving I may be...

3   If you should ever come to Cambridge, or near Head Quarters, I shall be happy to see a person so favour'd [well liked] by the Muses [inspirational forces]...

–G. Washington

Statue of Phillis Wheatley

Reread paragraph 1. **Circle** the reason why Wheatley is remembered. Write it here:

_____

_____

_____

Reread paragraph 2. **Underline** George Washington's description of Wheatley's poem.

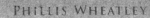
COLLABORATE

Talk with a partner about George Washington's letter to Wheatley. Did he indicate that he enjoyed her poem? How do you know? Write your answer here:

_____

_____

_____

_____

? What is the author's purpose for writing about the two poets?

Quick Tip

When you cite text evidence, you use the exact words or phrases from a selection you read in your response. The text evidence should support your answer.

Talk About It Reread the excerpts on pages 142 and 143. Talk with a partner about the accomplishments of the two poets.

Cite Text Evidence What words and phrases does the author use to describe each poet? Write text evidence in the chart.

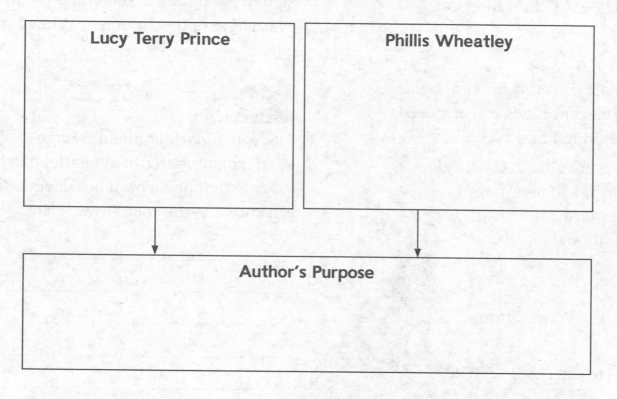

Lucy Terry Prince	Phillis Wheatley

Author's Purpose

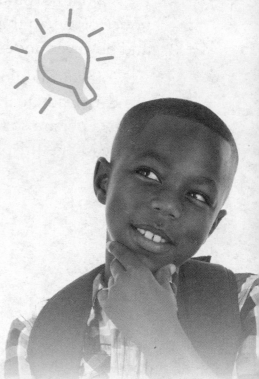

Write The author's purpose for writing about these two poets is _____

_____

_____

_____

CHECK IN 1 2 3 4

Print and Graphic Features

Writers include **print** and **graphic** features to make their pieces more interesting and to support the information. Some features include primary and secondary accounts, such as obituaries and letters from the time period. Other features, such as photos, help writers tell their story.

 FIND TEXT EVIDENCE

On page 142, paragraph 3 contains an excerpt from Lucy Terry Prince's obituary. The author includes this piece because it gives evidence of the respect Terry earned during her lifetime.

> *In this remarkable woman there was an assemblage of qualities rarely to be found...*

 Your Turn Reread paragraph 2 on page 143. Look at the photograph of the sculpture.

- How does George Washington's letter strengthen the idea that Phillis Wheatley was a notable poet? _____

_____

_____

- How does the sculpture of Phillis Wheatley support the author's position? _____

_____

CHECK IN ⟩ 1 ⟩ 2 ⟩ 3 ⟩ 4 ⟩

? **What do people do to solve problems?**

Talk About It Think about the selections you read. Look at the photograph and read the caption. Talk with a partner about what examples of problem solving you see in the photograph.

Cite Text Evidence With a partner, **draw arrows** pointing at three ideas that represent problem solving. **Circle** text evidence in the caption that tells one way.

Write The selections I read and this photograph help me understand how people solve problems by _____

_____

_____

_____

_____

_____

_____

This group of teachers hold a collaborative discussion about schoolwide issues.

CHECK IN 1 2 3 4

My Goal I know what good problem solvers do.

Create a Bookmark

Many people solved problems during the Revolutionary War and the formation of the U.S. Constitution. Think about how they succeeded. Create a bookmark that describes how to become good problem solvers.

1. Look at your Build Knowledge notes in your reader's notebook.

2. On one side of your bookmark, list three steps for how to be a good problem solver. On the other side of the bookmark, write a paragraph explaining why these steps are important to resolving problems.

3. Use evidence from the texts you read to support your ideas. Use new vocabulary words.

Think about what you learned in this text set. Fill in the bars on page 125.

Build Knowledge

? Essential Question

When has a plan helped you accomplish a task?

Build Vocabulary

Write new words you learned about some things you need to do when planning for a successful outcome for a task. Draw lines and circles for the words you write.

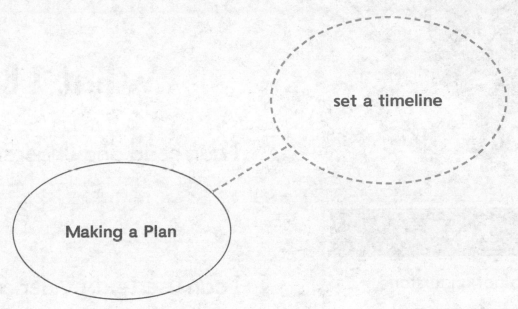

set a timeline

Making a Plan

Go online to **my.mheducation.com** and read the "Stand By Your Plan" Blast. Think about how long it took to build the Panama Canal. How do you think having a good plan helps make a huge project a success? Then blast back your response.

Think about what you already know. Fill in the bars. There are no wrong answers here.

What I Know Now

I can read and understand a folktale.

| 1 | 2 | 3 | 4 |

I can use text evidence to respond to a folktale.

| 1 | 2 | 3 | 4 |

I know how following a plan can help people accomplish a task.

| 1 | 2 | 3 | 4 |

Key
1 = I do not understand.
2 = I understand but need more practice.
3 = I understand.
4 = I understand and can teach someone.

 **STOP** You will come back to the next page later.

What I Learned

I can read and understand a folktale.

1 > 2 > 3 > 4

I can use text evidence to respond to a folktale.

1 > 2 > 3 > 4

I know how following a plan can help people accomplish a task.

1 > 2 > 3 > 4

My Goal
I can read and understand a folktale.

TAKE NOTES

As you read, make note of interesting words and important events.

The Magical Lost Brocade

Essential Question

?

When has a plan helped you accomplish a task?

Read about how Ping follows a plan to find a lost brocade.

Long ago, in China, a poor woman and her son, Ping, lived in a tiny hut. The woman earned a living weaving beautiful brocade hangings, which her son sold. She wished she could give Ping a better home, but alas, that was impossible. So she decided to weave a brocade of a magnificent house with gardens. At least they could look at something lovely. It took three years to complete the brocade, and it was her finest work. However, soon afterward, a great wind swept into their hut and carried it away! The woman was grief-stricken. So Ping went off in **pursuit** of the brocade, **assuring** his mother he would bring it home.

Ping walked for three days and came to a stone house. A bearded man sat outside. "I'm searching for my mother's brocade," Ping said.

"A brocade flew by three days ago," said the man. "Now it's in a palace far away. I'll explain how you can get there and lend you my horse." Ping thanked the man and bowed deeply to express his **gratitude.**

"First, you must ride through Fire Valley," said the man. "You must cross over it regardless of the scorching heat, without uttering a word. If you utter even a single sound, you'll burn!" He continued, "After you've crossed Fire Valley, you'll arrive at Ice Ocean. You must ride through the icy waters without shivering. If you shiver even once, the **outcome** will be terrible! The sea will swallow you up!" The old man paused before concluding, "When you emerge from the sea, you'll be facing the Mountain of the Sun. The mountain is as steep as a straight line up to the sky! The palace sits on top of the mountain, and the brocade is in the palace."

FIND TEXT EVIDENCE

Read

Paragraph 1
Make Predictions

Do you think Ping will find the brocade? Explain your answer.

_____

_____

Paragraphs 2–3
Theme

Underline a sentence that shows that Ping is grateful. What might the author's message be?

_____

_____

Paragraph 4
Plot: Setting

Circle the places that tell what kind of story this is.

Reread

Author's Craft

How does the author's use of imagery make you feel as you read the first part of Ping's journey?

Read

Paragraph 1
Theme

Underline the words Ping uses to describe the journey and what he will do. What is the author's message?

_____

_____

Paragraph 2
Personification

Circle the words that make Ice Ocean seem human.

Paragraphs 3–4
Make Inferences

Why do you think Princess Ling did not return the brocade herself?

_____

_____

Reread

Author's Craft

Why is Princess Ling's appearance important to the story?

"It sounds like an extremely difficult journey," said Ping, "but I'll do my very best." He mounted the horse and traveled for three days, reaching the Fire Valley. As he crossed the valley, angry flames leaped out at him. The intense heat brought tears to Ping's eyes, but he said nothing.

When he reached the other side of the valley, he saw the Ice Ocean. With Ping's gentle **guidance,** the horse entered the frigid waters. The sea touched Ping with icy fingers, but he didn't shiver once. So horse and rider crossed the sea, **emerging** safely on the other side.

Next, Ping approached the Mountain of the Sun. He rode up the steep mountain, grasping the reins for dear life! Finally, he reached the top and dismounted at the palace door.

A lovely princess welcomed him. "I'm Princess Ling," she said. "I thought your mother's brocade was beautiful and wanted to copy it. So I sent a great wind to your home. I've now copied the brocade, so please take it home. Have a safe journey."

"Thank you," said Ping, who stared at the beautiful princess. She was a perfect rose. He wondered if he could see her again and **detected** a knowing smile on her face as they said good-bye.

Ping mounted his horse, placing the brocade under his jacket. First, he rode down the steep Mountain of the Sun. Next, he rode back across Ice Ocean, without shivering once. Then he rode across Fire Valley, without making a sound. Finally, he arrived at the home of the bearded man, who sat outside just as he had the **previous** time. Ping thanked him, returned his horse, and began the long walk home.

Ping arrived home three days later. "Here is your brocade, Mother!" he announced as she cried tears of joy. Together, they unrolled it, and before their eyes, the brocade came to life! Suddenly their hut became a magnificent house with gardens. But that wasn't all—standing before them was Princess Ling! Ping and the princess got married, and a year later, Ping's mother became a loving grandmother. They all lived happily together in their beautiful home and gardens!

Summarize

Use your notes to orally summarize the plot and theme of "The Magical Lost Brocade."

FOLKTALE

FIND TEXT EVIDENCE

Read

Paragraph 1
Make Predictions

Do you think Ping will see Princess Ling again?

_____

_____

Underline a clue in the first paragraph that you used to make your prediction.

Paragraphs 2–3
Theme

What is the author's message at the end of the story?

_____

_____

Draw a box around the text evidence.

Reread

Author's Craft

Do you think the author's ending was a good one? Why or why not?

Vocabulary

Use the example sentences to talk with a partner about each word. Then answer the questions.

assuring

One job of coaching is **assuring** athletes that they will do well.

What might a coach say when assuring a team?

_____

_____

detected

By the way he sniffed, I knew my dog **detected** another animal.

What have you detected just by hearing?

_____

_____

emerging

I watched as the chick was **emerging** from its shell.

What word or phrase has the same meaning as *emerging*?

_____

_____

gratitude

I gave flowers to my aunt to show my **gratitude** for her help.

What is another way people show their gratitude?

_____

_____

guidance

With my Uncle Rico's **guidance**, I learned how to play the guitar.

Whose guidance has helped you learn a new skill?

_____

_____

 Build Your Word List Reread the fourth paragraph on page 153. Circle the word *arrive*. In your reader's notebook, use a word web to write more forms of the word. For example, write *arrival*. Use an online or print dictionary to check for accuracy.

outcome

The team was pleased with the **outcome** of the game.

When has the outcome of a game surprised you?

_____

_____

previous

My older brother was the **previous** owner of my bike as he had it before me.

What was the name of your previous teacher?

_____

_____

pursuit

On a nature show, I watched a lion in **pursuit** of a zebra.

What might a house cat be in pursuit of?

_____

_____

Personification

Writers sometimes use words in unusual ways to help you better picture an animal, a thing, or an event. **Personification** gives human qualities to an animal or object.

FIND TEXT EVIDENCE

When I read the sentence on page 153 "The sea will swallow you up!" I know the writer is using personification. The word swallow _gives the sea the action of a person._

"The sea will swallow you up!"

Your Turn The following sentence from "The Magical Lost Brocade" contains an example of personification. Explain how the example shows human qualities.

As he crossed the valley, angry flames leaped out at him, page 154 _____

_____

_____

CHECK IN 〉 1 〉 2 〉 3 〉 4 〉

Make Predictions

A prediction is a guess about what might happen. Making predictions helps you focus your reading. Use text evidence to see if your predictions are confirmed. If your predictions are not confirmed, you can correct them. This helps you monitor, or check, your understanding of the story.

 FIND TEXT EVIDENCE

After you read about the tasks Ping must do in order to find the brocade on page 154, you may want to predict whether or not he will succeed before you continue reading.

Page 154

"It sounds like an extremely difficult journey," said Ping, "but I'll do my very best." He mounted the horse and traveled for three days, reaching the Fire Valley. As he crossed the valley, angry flames leaped out at him. The intense heat brought tears to Ping's eyes, but he said nothing.

When he reached the other side of the valley, he saw the Ice Ocean. With Ping's gentle **guidance**, the horse entered the frigid waters. The sea touched Ping with icy fingers, but he didn't shiver once. So horse and rider crossed the sea, **emerging** safely on the other side.

> On page 154, Ping tells the old man, "It sounds like an extremely difficult journey, but I'll do my very best." I predicted Ping would succeed. As I continued reading, I saw my prediction was right.

Quick Tip

Your predictions should make sense based on the story's genre. For example, folktales often have magical events. You may predict that Ping will find something magical that will help him during his journey.

Your Turn Tell one prediction you made after Ping left the Mountain of the Sun. Was your prediction correct? If not, tell how you revised it based on your knowledge of folktales. _____

_____

_____

CHECK IN 1 2 3 4

Plot: Setting

In a **folktale**, a hero or heroine goes on a quest to accomplish a set of tasks. A folktale's setting is in the distant past. The cultural setting is often in a land specific to the people that created the story. You can analyze how the setting moves the plot forward by noting how the setting affects characters' actions and responses to events. Folktales may include elements such as repetition of actions or words, foreshadowing, and imagery.

Quick Tip

Sometimes words in a story do not give a full description of the setting. Looking at the illustrations can help you better understand the setting.

FIND TEXT EVIDENCE

I can tell that "The Magical Lost Brocade" is a folktale. It describes Ping's quest. It has elements of a folktale. It is set a long time ago in China.

Page 153

Long ago, in China, a poor woman and her son, Ping, lived in a tiny hut. The woman earned a living weaving beautiful brocade hangings, which her son sold. She wished she could give Ping a better home, but alas, that was impossible. So she decided to weave a brocade of a magnificent house with gardens. At least they could look at something lovely. It took three years to complete the brocade, and it was her finest work. However, soon afterward, a great wind swept into their hut and carried it away! The woman was grief-stricken. So Ping went off in **pursuit** of the brocade, **assuring** his mother he would bring it home.

Ping walked for three days and came to a stone house. A bearded man sat outside. "I'm searching for my mother's brocade," Ping said.

"A brocade flew by three days ago," said the man. "Now it's in a palace far away. I'll explain how you can get there and lend you my horse." Ping thanked the man and bowed deeply to express his **gratitude**.

"First, you must ride through Fire Valley," said the man. "You must cross over it regardless of the scorching heat, without uttering a word. If you utter even a single sound, you'll burn!" He continued, "After you've crossed Fire Valley, you'll arrive at Ice Ocean. You must ride through the icy waters without shivering. If you shiver even once, the **outcome** will be terrible! The sea will swallow you up!" The old man paused before concluding, "When you emerge from the sea, you'll be facing the Mountain of the Sun. The mountain is as steep as a straight line up to the sky! The palace sits on top of the mountain, and the brocade is in the palace."

Setting

The story takes place long ago in China.

Foreshadowing

Foreshadowing gives readers clues about the outcome of events in a story.

Your Turn List clues about this folktale's cultural setting. Then state how the setting impacts the plot events.

COLLABORATE

_____

_____

_____

_____

_____

CHECK IN 1 2 3 4

Theme

The theme of a story is an overall idea or message about life that the author wants to share. Themes may be stated directly or implied. To find an implied theme, think about the plot, setting, and what the characters think, say, or do. A character's perspective can help to develop a theme.

 FIND TEXT EVIDENCE

At the end of the first paragraph on page 153, Ping assures his mother he will find her brocade. I know Ping cares about his mother and wants to make her feel better. I can use Ping's perspective to find the theme.

What Does the Character Think, Say, or Do?	What Is the Character's Perspective?
Ping assures his mother he will find her lost brocade and goes off to search for it.	Ping cares about his mother and doesn't want her to be sad about her lost brocade.

Theme
Family members care about and help each other.

 Your Turn Reread "The Magical Lost Brocade." Complete the graphic organizer on page 161 to determine another theme of the story. Record what Ping thinks, says, and does and then his perspective. State the theme you inferred.

CHECK IN ⟩ 1 ⟩ 2 ⟩ 3 ⟩ 4 ⟩

**What Does the Character
Think, Say, or Do?**

**What Is the Character's
Perspective?**

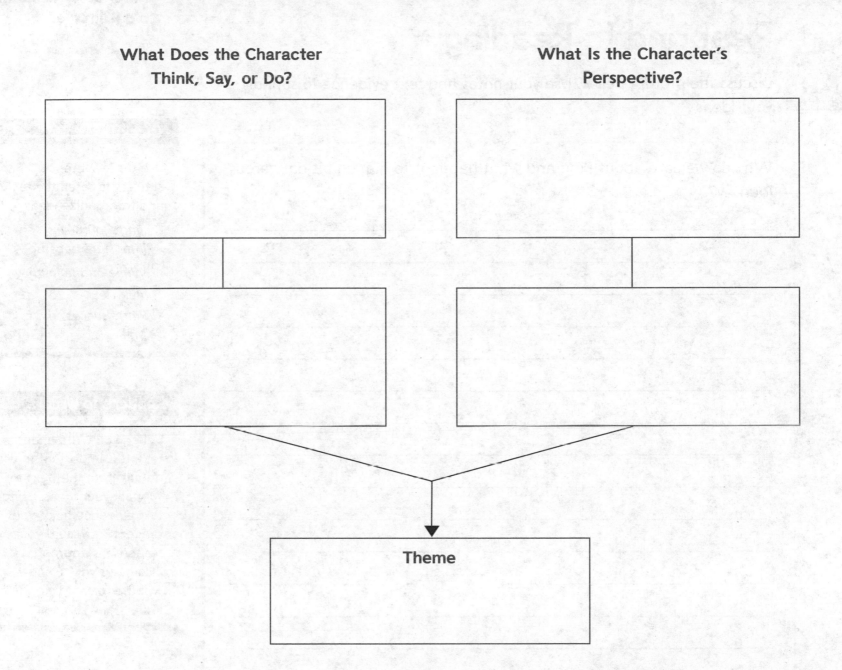

Theme

Respond to Reading

COLLABORATE

Discuss the prompt below. Use your notes and text evidence to support your ideas.

Why do we care about Ping and what happens to him on his dangerous journey?

_____

_____

_____

_____

_____

_____

_____

_____

_____

_____

_____

_____

Quick Tip

Use these sentence starters to retell the text and to organize ideas.

- *Ping's journey is important because . . .*
- *While on the journey, Ping . . .*
- *Ping's success shows that . . .*

Readers to Writers

When you write about a text, it is important to use details from that text to support your ideas. Using text evidence helps your readers know that your response is appropriate. It also helps you to know whether or not you understand the text.

CHECK IN 1 〉 2 〉 3 〉 4 〉

Accomplishing a Task

A good research plan indicates a project's purpose and the steps needed to complete the plan. Follow the research process to make an illustrated food web that shows the flow of energy among producers, consumers, and decomposers. Work collaboratively within a group.

Step 1 **Set a Goal** Develop a logical plan for collecting information about a food web. Create and define roles for each person in your group.

Step 2 **Identify Sources** Use books, magazines, and websites to find information and visuals to include in your illustrated food web. Make a list of other sources you might use.

_____

_____

Step 3 **Find and Record Information** Collect relevant information from your sources and take notes. Compare and contrast how plants and animals are connected in your food web. Cite your sources.

Step 4 **Organize and Synthesize Information** Make a rough sketch of your food web. Organize the illustrations and accompanying text into a flowchart.

Step 5 **Create and Present** Create a final illustrated food web. Be sure the illustrations clearly relate to the text and are easy to follow. Think about how you will present your food web to the class.

Project: Illustrated Food Web

Materials: notebook, reference sources

Step 1. Arrange with a teacher for a walk outdoors.

What do you think would be a logical Step 2 for the above plan?

_____

_____

_____

CHECK IN 1 2 3 4

Blancaflor

*Literature Anthology:
pages 118-131*

? How does the author use personification to set the mood of the story?

COLLABORATE

Talk About It Reread **Literature Anthology** page 119. Turn to your partner and discuss how the author describes the tree.

Cite Text Evidence What phrases describe the tree and set the mood of the folktale? Write text evidence in the chart.

Evidence	Mood

Evaluate Information

Authors use figurative language in folktales to create memorable stories. A simile compares things using *like* or *as*. A metaphor compares things without using *like* or *as*. Personification gives human qualities to nonhuman things. Why do you think it was appropriate or not for the author of this folktale to use personification?

Write The author uses personification to _____

_____

CHECK IN   1   2   3   4

How does the author use descriptive language to help you visualize what the prince is experiencing?

 Talk About It Reread the first two paragraphs on **Literature Anthology** page 123. Talk to a partner about how the author describes the landscape and what happens to the prince.

Cite Text Evidence What phrases create imagery? Use this web to record text evidence.

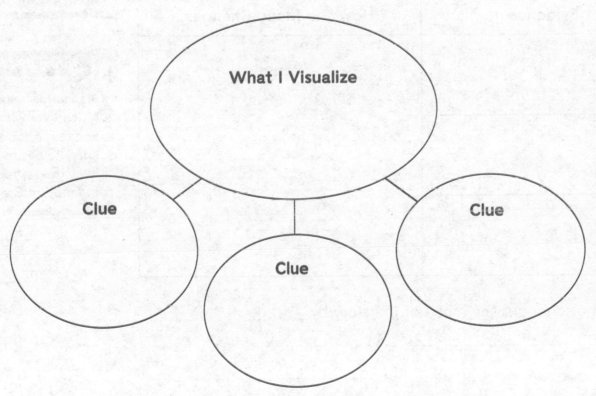

What I Visualize

Clue

Clue

Clue

Clue

Write I can visualize the setting because the author _____

_____

_____

Quick Tip

The author uses phrases such as *deserted and barren* and *basalt and obsidian*. You can use context clues to help you understand what the phrases mean. For example, *deserted* describes a barren, or empty, place.

 Evaluate Information

Details in the story can help you determine the setting. The setting can influence the plot. For example, a story set in a desert may have characters trying to find water in order to survive. How does the setting of *Blancaflor* affect what Alfonso does?

CHECK IN 1 2 3 4

? **How does the author use words and phrases to change the mood of the story?**

Talk About It Reread paragraphs 3-6 on **Literature Anthology** page 130. Turn to a partner and discuss how the mood of the folktale changes.

Cite Text Evidence What phrases mark the climax, or turning point, of the story? Write them in the chart and describe how the mood changes.

Text Evidence	How the Mood Changes

Write The author changes the mood of the story by _____

_____

_____

Quick Tip

Mood refers to the emotions the reader feels. Mood is set by the author's word choices. For example, a story's mood can be either cheerful or sad. Look at how the story's mood changes after specific plot events.

Make Inferences

Blancaflor helps Alfonso in his conflict with her father. She tells Alfonso which horse to use to escape. Why does Alfonso choose the other horse instead?

CHECK IN 1 2 3 4

Respond to Reading

COLLABORATE

Discuss the prompt below. Use your notes and text evidence to support your response.

Why is it important for people to keep their word?

_____

_____

_____

_____

_____

_____

_____

_____

_____

_____

_____

_____

Quick Tip

Use these sentence starters to paraphrase the text and to help organize your text evidence.

- _Alfonso feels that . . ._

- _The author uses figurative language to show . . ._

- _The author uses descriptions of. . ._

CHECK IN ❯ 1 ❯ 2 ❯ 3 ❯ 4 ❯

From Tale to Table

Literature Anthology:
pages 134-137

1   Whether it's a princess turning into a dove or a frog turning into a prince, many folktales and fairy tales include a magical transformation of one thing into another. Though it seems like an impossible task that only a magician could do, transformations can in fact happen in real life—even in your own kitchen!

A Wise Plan

2   Through the process of cooking and baking, individual ingredients can be transformed into something delicious. Did you know that the bread in the sandwich you had for lunch was probably made with only six basic ingredients: flour, water, oil, yeast, salt, and sugar? It may seem impossible, but by combining and heating these ingredients you can create something different: bread. It's not magic, but it does require a plan.

Reread paragraph 1. **Circle** clues that show what the author does to help you understand what a transformation is. Then **underline** what the author thinks of transformations. Write it here:

_____

_____

_____

COLLABORATE

Reread paragraph 2. Talk with your partner about what you have to do to transform ingredients into bread. **Write** the numbers 1 to 6 beside each ingredient.

Then **draw a box** around what the author uses to foreshadow what information comes next.

(bkgd) Dave King/Dorling Kindersley/Getty Images

168   Unit 2 • Text Set 2

Too Hot, Too Cold, and Just Right

1   A recipe has usually been tried and tested previously, so it is important to follow the steps carefully to get the same result. Slight changes in temperature can affect the outcome. For example, in step 1, the water should be warm, not hot. Why? Though it's hard to tell by looking at it, yeast is a living organism. At the right temperature, it gives off gases that create bubbles in the dough. This is what makes the dough rise. If you use hot water in the recipe, you can kill the yeast. If you use cold water, the yeast may create very little or no gas. Without the gas that the yeast produces, the dough will not rise.

Reread the excerpt. **Underline** what the author thinks is important to do when using a recipe. **Circle** something that might happen if you don't do it.

COLLABORATE

Talk with a partner about how the author uses cause and effect to organize information. Place **a mark** in the margin beside each cause-and-effect relationship in the paragraph. Write one of them here:

_____

_____

_____

_____

? Why is "From Tale to Table" a good title for this selection?

COLLABORATE

Talk About It Reread paragraph 1 on page 168. Talk with a partner about how the author introduces the selection and why that introduction is important.

Cite Text Evidence How does the author connect tales and recipes? Write text evidence in the chart.

Synthesize Information

Combine what you know about folktales with information in "From Tale to Table." Why does the author of "From Tale to Table" use "magical transformation" in the introduction?

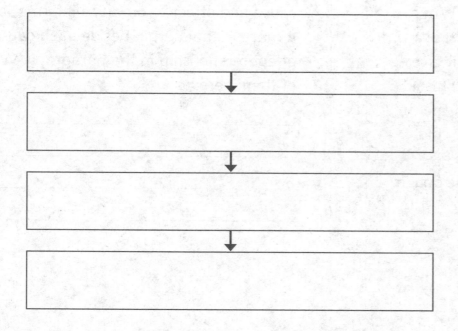

Write "From Tale to Table" is a good title for this

selection because _____

_____

_____

_____

CHECK IN   1   2   3   4

Sequence

Text structure includes the way an author organizes information or ideas for the readers. An author of a procedure or process may use an organizational pattern such as sequential order, or order of importance.

FIND TEXT EVIDENCE

In the second paragraph of "From Tale to Table" on page 168, the author discusses the process of cooking and baking. The author organizes the text logically in a sequential order by giving an example of bread and stating that the process begins with the ingredients.

> Did you know that the bread in the sandwich you had for lunch was probably made with only |six basic ingredients:| flour, water, oil, yeast, salt, and sugar?

Your Turn Reread the text on page 169 in the section "Too Hot, Too Cold, and Just Right."

- In this section, how does the author organize the text in a sequential order?

  _____

  _____

- Why does this organizational pattern make sense? _____

  _____

  _____

CHECK IN 1 > 2 > 3 > 4 >

? How do the Wright brothers and the authors of *Blancaflor* and "From Tale to Table" help you understand how plans can help people accomplish a task?

Talk About It Look at the sketches and read the caption. Talk with a partner about each image and what they tell you about the Wright brothers.

Cite Text Evidence Circle three things in the sketches that show how the Wright brothers planned to build their flying machine. Think about why the Wright brothers drew up these plans. In the margin beside each sketch, write words that describe the plans.

Write The Wright brothers and the authors show

_____

_____

_____

_____

_____

_____

_____

George Grantham Bain Collection (Library of Congress)

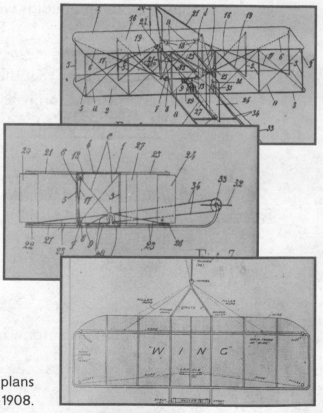

The Wright brothers drew up these plans for their flying machine in 1908.

CHECK IN 1 2 3 4

Create a Recipe for Success

What do the characters you read about have in common? Write a recipe for accomplishing a task.

1. Look at your Build Knowledge notes in your reader's notebook.

2. Make a list of ingredients for your recipe. Use evidence from the texts to explain what the characters have in common.

3. Write at least three steps. Then write a paragraph describing why following these steps is necessary for accomplishing a task. Use new vocabulary words.

Think about what you learned in this text set. Fill in the bars on page 151.

Build Knowledge

Essential Question

What motivates you to accomplish a goal?

Build Vocabulary

Write new words you learned about what it takes to achieve a goal. Draw lines and circles for the words you write.

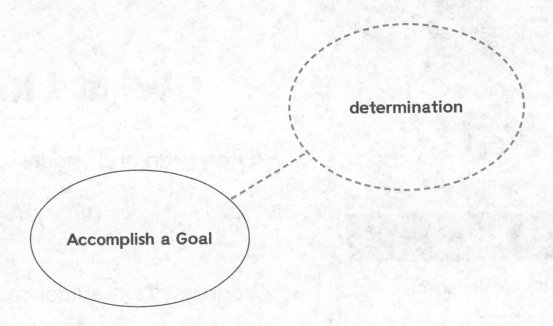

determination

Accomplish a Goal

Go online to **my.mheducation.com** and read the "Reaching a Goal" Blast. When was the last time you had a goal that you tried to reach? Did you reach it? How did you know when you had reached your goal? Then blast back your response.

Ruth Jenkinson/Dorling Kindersley/Getty Images

Think about what you already know. Fill in the bars. You'll keep learning more.

What I Know Now

Key	
1 =	I do not understand.
2 =	I understand but need more practice.
3 =	I understand.
4 =	I understand and can teach someone.

I can read and understand poetry.

1 > 2 > 3 > 4

I can use text evidence to respond to poetry.

1 > 2 > 3 > 4

I know what motivates people to accomplish a goal.

1 > 2 > 3 > 4

STOP You will come back to the next page later.

Think about what you learned. Fill in the bars. Keep up the good work!

What I Learned

I can read and understand poetry.

1 > 2 > 3 > 4

I can use text evidence to respond to poetry.

1 > 2 > 3 > 4

I know what motivates people to accomplish a goal.

1 > 2 > 3 > 4

My Goal

I can read and understand poetry.

TAKE NOTES

Make note of interesting words and important details.

_____

_____

_____

_____

_____

_____

_____

_____

_____

_____

_____

_____

_____

A Simple Plan

Each morning when Jack rises,
He schemes a simple plot:
"I think I'll change the world," says he,
"A little, not a lot."
For neighbors he might mow a lawn
Before they know he's done it,
Or lead a soccer match at school,
And not care which team won it.
Some kids would laugh,
but Jack would smile
And look for more to do.
He'd walk your dog or tell a joke,
Or play a song for you.
Jack's brother John just didn't see
What Jack was all about.
John shuddered at Jack's crazy ways,
But Jack had not one doubt.

Essential Question

?

What motivates you to accomplish a goal?

Read how two poets describe unusual goals and why they matter.

"Who wants to do another's chores?"
John asked. "What does it mean,
'I'll change the world?' You're wasting time.
What changes have you seen?"
"Little brother," Jack explained,
"I used to think like you.
I thought, 'Why bother?' and 'Who cares?'
I see you do that, too.
I'd see some grass not mowed, or else
Kids not getting along,
And in the park no games to play—
I'd wonder what was wrong.
And then I had to ask myself,
What was I waiting for?
The change can start with me, you see,
That key is in my door.
I've memorized a thousand names,
And everyone knows me.
What do *you* do?" John had to think.
And he began to see.
Now each morning when Jack rises,
He hears his brother plan:
"I think I'll change the world," says John,
"If I can't, then who can?"

— Peter Collier

(bkgd) Peter Zander/Photolibrary/Getty Images; (r)Fancy/Alamy

FIND TEXT EVIDENCE

Read

Pages 178–179

Repetition

Draw a box around the words *I'll change the world*. Who says this the first time? Who says it the second time? Who says it the last time?

_____

_____

_____

Page 179

Theme

By the end of the poem, what lesson has John learned? **Underline** the text evidence.

_____

_____

_____

Reread

Author's Craft

How does the repetition in this poem help create a theme?

FIND TEXT EVIDENCE

Read

▼

Page 180

Homographs

Circle the context clues that help you determine the meaning of the word *tipped*. Write the meaning.

_____

_____

Page 180

Theme

Underline details about the effect of the oil spill on the birds. What do they tell you about how the speaker feels?

_____

_____

_____

_____

_____

_____

Reread

▼

Author's Craft

How does the poet help you visualize the effect of the spill?

RESCUE

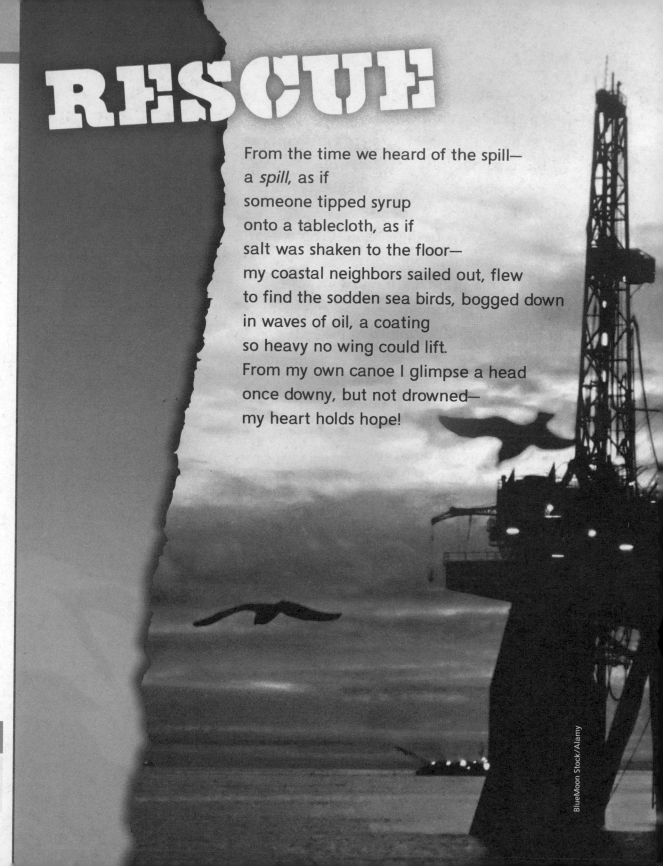

From the time we heard of the spill—
a *spill*, as if
someone tipped syrup
onto a tablecloth, as if
salt was shaken to the floor—
my coastal neighbors sailed out, flew
to find the sodden sea birds, bogged down
in waves of oil, a coating
so heavy no wing could lift.
From my own canoe I glimpse a head
once downy, but not drowned—
my heart holds hope!

BlueMoon Stock/Alamy

Reach, lift, and up—
it beats, this bird's heart!
I hold the sickened seagull, know:
Just as one spill can spell disaster,
One boat can bring back life.

— Elena Ruiz

Make Connections

Compare the speakers' feelings in the poems to the feelings you have when you try to accomplish a goal. Use your notes to explain what you learned from these poems.

FIND TEXT EVIDENCE

Read

Page 181

Free Verse

Free verse poems don't group words by rhyme. They group words to emphasize meaning. **Underline** the first line. What might the speaker be emphasizing?

_____

_____

_____

Theme

Draw a box around the last two lines on page 181. What is a meaning of these lines?

_____

_____

_____

Reread

Author's Craft

How would the poem be different if the speaker had told about the spill as an observer instead of a rescuer?

Vocabulary

Use the example sentences to talk with a partner about each word. Then answer the questions.

ambitious

Paulo is an **ambitious** bike rider and always looks for challenges.

What makes someone ambitious?

_____

_____

memorized

Pat **memorized** the poem and recited it perfectly for the class.

What is the name of a poem or song that you memorized?

_____

_____

satisfaction

Participating in sports, such as basketball, gave Jason great **satisfaction**.

What activity gives you great satisfaction?

_____

_____

shuddered

Jill **shuddered** as she bit into the tart, juicy lemon.

What is a synonym for *shuddered*?

_____

_____

Poetry Terms

narrative

I like to read **narrative** poems because they tell a story.

What story would you like to tell in a narrative poem?

_____

_____

repetition

The **repetition** of words, phrases, or lines is used for emphasis.

What is the repetition of a word or phrase that you would use to emphasize happiness?

_____

_____

free verse

A **free verse** poem does not have a set rhyming pattern.

What topic would you choose for a free verse poem?

_____

_____

rhyme

A poem with **rhyme** contains words that end with the same sound.

Can you think of three words that rhyme with _funny_?

_____

_____

_____

Build Your Word List Reread "Rescue" on pages 180–181. Underline three adjectives. In your reader's notebook, write the three words. Use an online or print thesaurus to find two synonyms for each word. Write the synonyms next to each adjective.

Homographs

Homographs are words that are spelled the same but have different meanings and may or may not have the same pronunciation. You can use context clues to help figure out which meaning is correct.

FIND TEXT EVIDENCE

In "A Simple Plan," I see the word park. _I know that_ park _can be a verb meaning "to place or leave something" and it can also be a noun meaning "land set apart for recreation." The phrase "games to play" is a clue that_ park _has the second meaning._

> I'd see some grass not mowed, or else
> Kids not getting along,
> And in the park no games to play—
> I'd wonder what was wrong.

Your Turn Reread the homographs _down_ and _spell_ in the poem "Rescue." Identify clues that help you figure out the meaning. Use a print or digital dictionary to check your work.

_____

_____

_____

CHECK IN ▶ 1 ⟩ 2 ⟩ 3 ⟩ 4 ⟩

Repetition and Rhyme

Poets may use **repetition**, or the repeated use of words, sounds, or phrases, for effect. Repeating a word, phrase, or sentence style helps emphasize the meaning. Words **rhyme** when their endings sound the same.

 FIND TEXT EVIDENCE

Reread the poem "Rescue" on pages 180 and 181. Look for phrases and words that are repeated and note the effect they create.

> ### Quick Tip
> Words that rhyme don't always end with the same spelling. To hear and identify the rhyming words, try reading the poem out loud. Reading aloud will also help you hear a rhyming pattern.

Page 180

From the time we heard of the spill—
a *spill*, as if
someone tipped syrup
onto a tablecloth, as if
salt was shaken to the floor—
my coastal neighbors sailed out, flew
to find the sodden sea birds, bogged down
in waves of oil, a coating
so heavy no wing could lift.

The word spill *is repeated to emphasize the event. The words* as if *are repeated to emphasize that the spill in the poem is worse than spilling syrup or salt.*

Your Turn Find two examples of repetition in "A Simple Plan" and tell what is being emphasized.

1 _____

_____

2 _____

_____

CHECK IN ❯ 1 ❯ 2 ❯ 3 ❯ 4 ❯

Narrative and Free Verse

Narrative poetry tells a story. It has characters and can have dialogue. Narrative poetry can rhyme but does not have to.

Free verse shares ideas and feelings with no set rhyming pattern or rhythm. It has no set line length.

🔍 FIND TEXT EVIDENCE

I can tell that "A Simple Plan" is a narrative poem because it tells a story and has dialogue between characters. I see that "Rescue" is free verse because there is no set line length or rhyming pattern.

Page 179

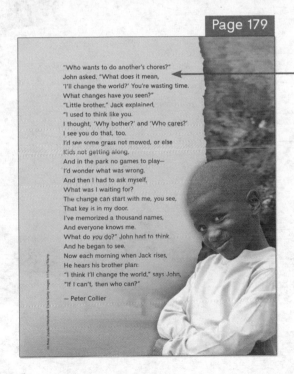

"Who wants to do another's chores?"
John asked. "What does it mean,
'I'll change the world?' You're wasting time.
What changes have you seen?"
"Little brother," Jack explained,
"I used to think like you.
I thought, 'Why bother?' and 'Who cares?'
I see you do that, too.
I'd see some grass not mowed, or else
Kids not getting along,
And in the park no games to play—
I'd wonder what was wrong.
And then I had to ask myself,
What was I waiting for?
The change can start with me, you see,
That key is in my door.
I've memorized a thousand names,
And everyone knows me.
What do *you* do?" John had to think
And he began to see.
Now each morning when Jack rises,
He hears his brother plan:
"I think I'll change the world," says John,
"If I can't, then who can?"

— Peter Collier

"A Simple Plan" is a narrative poem because it tells a story, has characters, and includes dialogue. Like some narrative poems, this one also rhymes.

COLLABORATE

Your Turn Reread the poems "A Simple Plan" and "Rescue." How does the choice to rhyme or not to rhyme affect the poems?

_____

_____

_____

_____

_____

CHECK IN   1   2   3   4

Theme

The **theme** is the big idea or message that the poet wishes to share. Thinking about the speaker, word choices, and important details that the poet uses and builds upon can help you develop the poem's theme.

🔍 FIND TEXT EVIDENCE

Both poems are about accomplishing goals, but each poem has a specific theme. I'll reread "A Simple Plan," think about who is speaking, and look for important details to figure out the poem's theme.

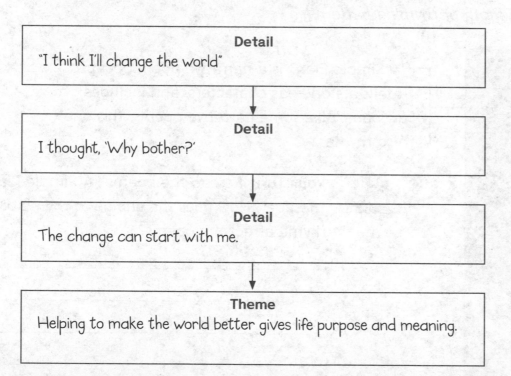

Detail
"I think I'll change the world"

↓

Detail
I thought, 'Why bother?'

↓

Detail
The change can start with me.

↓

Theme
Helping to make the world better gives life purpose and meaning.

Your Turn Reread the poem "Rescue." Think about the speaker and list important details in the graphic organizer on page 187. Use these details to figure out the poem's theme.

COLLABORATE

CHECK IN ⟩ 1 ⟩ 2 ⟩ 3 ⟩ 4

Peter Zander/Workbook Stock/Getty Images

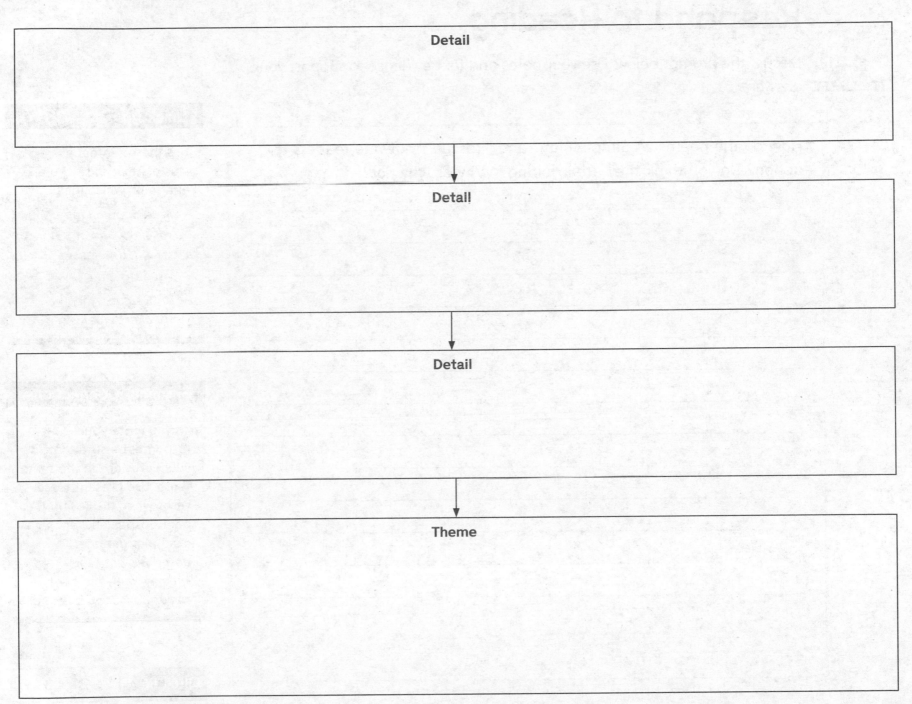

Detail

Detail

Detail

Theme

Respond to Reading

Discuss the prompt below. Use your notes and text evidence to support your answer.

How do the poems "A Simple Plan" and "Rescue" motivate readers to action? Do you think they are inspiring? Why or why not?

_____

_____

_____

_____

_____

_____

_____

_____

_____

_____

CHECK IN 1 2 3 4

Achieving Goals

Motivation is one of the biggest factors in accomplishing a goal. Follow the research process to create a comic strip showing how a prominent person or group from your state's history was able to achieve an important goal. Work with a partner.

Step 1 **Set a Goal** Brainstorm a list of famous people or groups from your state's history.

_____

_____

Step 2 **Identify Sources** Use primary and secondary sources such as books and websites to find information to incorporate into your comic strip.

Step 3 **Find and Record Information** Take notes specific to the goal that was achieved by the person or group you selected. Review photographs or other visuals to use as reference materials when you sketch your comic strip.

Step 4 **Organize and Synthesize Information** Analyze the information you gathered and organize it to help you sketch a story map.

Step 5 **Create and Present** Create your comic strip. Decide how you would like to present it to the class.

Quick Tip

Consider generating questions to help you determine who to pick from your brainstormed list and what to include in your comic strip. For example, you might ask: _What was their goal? What significant event occurred?_

What other questions can you think of that might help you?

_____

_____

_____

_____

_____

_____

CHECK IN ⟩ 1 ⟩ 2 ⟩ 3 ⟩ 4 ⟩

Stage Fright

Literature Anthology:
pages 138–140

? How does the poet structure the poem to help you understand how the speaker feels before and after he performs?

COLLABORATE

Talk About It Reread pages 138–139 in the **Literature Anthology.** Talk to your partner about how the poet sets the lines of the poem and how they relate to how the speaker feels.

Cite Text Evidence What does the poet write to help you visualize what the speaker is feeling? Write text evidence in the chart.

Evaluate Information

Notice the way the structure and appearance of the poem change in the middle and at the end. How do these sections relate to each other?

What the Poet Writes	What I Visualize

Write The poet helps me understand how the speaker feels by _____

_____

_____

CHECK IN 1 ⟩ 2 ⟩ 3 ⟩ 4

Catching Quiet

Why does the poet use repetition in "Catching Quiet"?

Talk About It Reread page 140 in the **Literature Anthology**. Turn to your partner and discuss the words and phrases the poet repeats.

Cite Text Evidence What words and phrases are repeated? Cite text evidence and explain why the poet repeats them.

Words and Phrases	Author's Purpose

Write The poet uses repetition in "Catching Quiet" to _____

_____

_____

_____

CHECK IN 1 2 3 4

My Goal I can use text evidence to respond to poetry.

Respond to Reading

COLLABORATE Discuss the prompt below. Use your notes and text evidence to support your answer.

What is the poet's message in each poem? How does that message motivate you to accomplish a goal?

_____

_____

_____

_____

_____

_____

_____

_____

_____

_____

_____

_____

_____

_____

_____

_____

Quick Tip

Use these sentence starters to help organize your text evidence.

• In "Stage Fright" the poet uses . . .

• In "Catching Quiet" the poet . . .

• This message is important because . . .

CHECK IN 1 2 3 4

Foul Shot

? How does the poet use personification to help you understand how the boy feels?

Literature Anthology: pages 142–143

COLLABORATE

Talk About It Reread page 142 in the **Literature Anthology**. Turn to your partner and talk about how the poet describes what the boy is feeling.

Cite Text Evidence What words and phrases help you create mental images of how the boy feels? Write text evidence in the chart.

Quick Tip

Use the word *person* in "personification" to help you remember meaning. *Personification* means giving human qualities to an animal or object.

Personification	How the Boy Feels

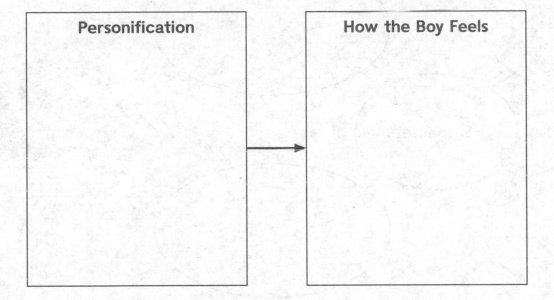

Write The poet uses personification to help me understand _____

_____

_____

_____

CHECK IN 1 2 3 4

? How does the poet's word choice create suspense in "Foul Shot"?

Quick Tip

Reading the poem out loud with expression will help you hear the words and phrases that create suspense.

COLLABORATE

Talk About It Reread page 143 in the **Literature Anthology**. With a partner, talk about what happens when the boy lets the basketball go.

Cite Text Evidence What words and phrases create a feeling of suspense in the poem? Write text evidence in the web.

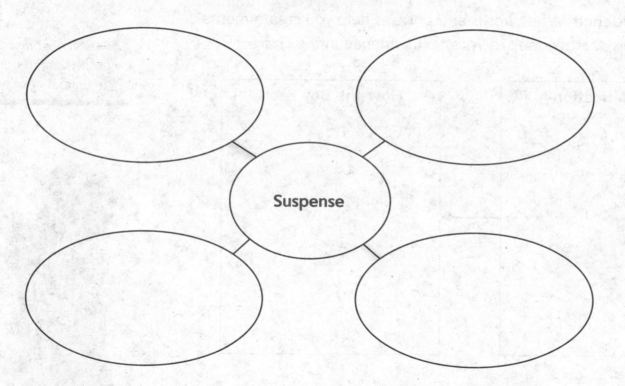

Suspense

Write The poet creates suspense by using words and phrases to _____

_____

_____

CHECK IN 1 2 3 4

Form and Line Breaks

In a poem, elements such as form, line breaks, and language work together to create voice. Voice gives the speaker a specific personality. To determine the voice, analyze the poem's form, or structure, of line breaks, line lengths, and stanzas. Notice where words are placed to create a specific effect. Paying attention to the words at the beginning and the end of a line can help you understand the emotions the poet wants to convey. For example, the words the poet chooses can make the voice in the poem sound happy, sad, excited, or lonely.

Readers to Writers

Think about how the speaker in the poem is feeling. When writing your own poem, consider language, line lengths, line breaks, rhyming patterns, and sentence structures that will best convey the speaker's feelings.

FIND TEXT EVIDENCE

Read aloud "Foul Shot" on pages 142–143 in the **Literature Anthology**. Think about how the speaker describes what is happening. On page 143, many of the lines have only one word. This stretches out the moments before the ball drops, creating suspense. The voice in these lines sounds very excited and focused on the game.

Your Turn Reread lines 11–13 on page 143.

• How are these lines different than the rest of the poem? _____

_____

_____

• How do these lines contribute to the voice in the poem? _____

_____

_____

CHECK IN 1 > 2 > 3 > 4 >

? How do the photograph and the poems "Stage Fright" and "Foul Shot" show how crowds or audiences can motivate players' performance?

COLLABORATE

Talk About It Look at the photograph and read the caption. With a partner, discuss whether you think the crowd will motivate the athlete and her teammates.

Cite Text Evidence **Underline** clues in the photograph that show what might motivate the athlete. **Circle** details that show how she feels.

Write I can see how a crowd can motivate a player's

performance because _____

_____

_____

_____

_____

_____

_____

_____

A soccer player runs through a line of people waiting on the sidelines to greet the team.

Quick Tip

Picture the audience in the poems "Stage Fright" and "Foul Shot." Compare them to the crowd interacting with the athlete and her teammates in the photo. What do they all have in common? You can use these words when you are making a comparison: *alike, and, both, similiar, same.*

CHECK IN ⟩ 1 ⟩ 2 ⟩ 3 ⟩ 4

My Goal I know what motivates people to accomplish a goal.

Write a Poem

You learned about many people who reached their goals. Think about how they accomplished them. What motivated these people to succeed?

1. Look at your Build Knowledge notes in your reader's notebook.

2. Write a free verse poem about why motivation is important to accomplishing a goal. Use text evidence to support your ideas.

3. Reread your poem. What ideas about motivation do you want to express clearly? Use some of the new words you learned. Be sure to include examples of repetition to emphasize certain feelings.

Think about what you learned in this text set. Fill in the bars on page 177.

Think about what you already know. Fill in the bars. Meeting your goals may take time.

Key
1 = I do not understand.
2 = I understand but need more practice.
3 = I understand.
4 = I understand and can teach someone.

What I Know Now

I can write an expository essay.

1 > 2 > 3 > 4

I can synthesize information from three sources.

1 > 2 > 3 > 4

Think about what you learned.
Fill in the bars. What do you want to
work on more?

What I Learned

I can write an expository essay.

1 > 2 > 3 > 4

I can synthesize information
from three sources.

1 > 2 > 3 > 4

WRITE TO SOURCES

You will answer an expository prompt using sources and a rubric.

ANALYZE THE RUBRIC

A rubric tells you what needs to be included in your writing.

Purpose, Focus, and Organization

Read the second bullet. What is a central idea?

A central idea is _____

_____

Evidence and Elaboration

Read the first bullet. How are facts and details connected to the central idea?

_____

_____

_____

_____

Evidence and Elaboration

Underline the word or words in the second bullet that tell you where the evidence comes from.

Expository Writing Rubric

Purpose, Focus, and Organization • Score 4

- stays focused on the purpose, audience, and task
- **clearly presents and fully develops the central idea about a topic**
- uses transitional strategies, such as words and phrases, to connect ideas
- uses a logical text structure to organize information
- begins with a strong introduction and ends with a strong conclusion

Evidence and Elaboration • Score 4

- effectively supports the central idea with convincing facts and details
- has strong examples of relevant evidence, or supporting details, from multiple sources
- uses elaborative techniques, such as facts, examples, definitions, and quotations from sources
- expresses interesting ideas clearly using precise language
- uses appropriate academic and domain-specific language
- uses different sentence structures

Turn to page 240 for the complete Expository Writing Rubric.

Central Idea

Present the Central Idea A strong expository essay presents a clear central idea. Read the paragraph below. The central idea is highlighted.

What does the central idea tell you about the focus of the essay?

Purpose

Writers think about their purpose when they write. They make choices about the facts and examples they use to support their ideas. Reread the paragraph about Edison, Ford, and Firestone's plan. What do you think is the author's purpose for writing?

> In the early 1900s, the United States imported rubber from overseas. Thomas Edison, Henry Ford, and Harvey Firestone had an idea that resulted from the United States' reliance on this foreign rubber. They feared that the foreign rubber would not be as accessible one day. They sought to find a local plant that had enough latex, or rubber, and could grow quickly. They founded a laboratory where Edison could test plant samples from all over the East Coast. The laboratory often had many visitors. **Their plan had an immediate effect on the rubber industry.**

_____

_____

_____

Details Writers use relevant details to support and develop their central idea. Details should help keep the essay focused on the central idea. Strong writers do not include unimportant details in their writing.

Read the paragraph above. Cross out an unimportant detail that does NOT maintain the central idea.

WRITING

ANALYZE THE STUDENT MODEL

Paragraph 1

Write a detail from Keya's introduction that caught your attention.

_____

_____

_____

Read the first paragraph of Keya's essay. The central idea is highlighted.

Paragraph 2

What is an example of relevant evidence, or detail, that Keya uses to support her central idea? **Circle** an example of elaboration. How does this further support Keya's central idea?

_____

_____

_____

_____

_____

Student Model: Expository Essay

Keya responded to the Writing Prompt: _Write an expository essay to present to your class about how women solved problems during the American Revolution._ Read Keya's essay below.

1   In the 1770s, America's fight for independence was not equal. Women couldn't speak out or fight. Back then, I wouldn't have been allowed to say anything! But three brave colonial women solved problems when women couldn't voice their opinions or participate in government.

2   When men were at the Continental Congress, Abigail Adams wanted to speak out about women's formal education and slavery. Adams solved her problem by sharing her opinions in letters to her husband. John Adams was a lawmaker with the Continental Congress. In one letter from August 1776, she wrote, "If we mean to have Heroes, Statesmen, and Philosophers, we should have learned women." Educated women belonged alongside the men. According to "Abigail Adams, Early Supporter of Equal Rights," the delegates didn't "prioritize these rights." But Abigail Adams used letter writing to solve her problem.

3   Martha Washington was another woman who solved problems. As General George Washington's wife, she didn't like being alone while he was leading the Continental Army. So she packed a bag and joined George at Valley Forge when the fighting paused. While at the camp, she ran the household, ordered supplies, and organized meals, says the article "The Women of Valley Forge." This helped George focus on the military. The article also says that other wives joined their husbands. They helped improve morale. When the fighting began again, the soldiers were stronger and more determined.

4   The women at Valley Forge helped soldiers. But Deborah Sampson became a soldier! During the war, women couldn't be soldiers. But Sampson wanted to fight. She solved this problem by pretending to be a man. According to "America's First Woman Soldier," the uniform hid her figure, and Sampson became Private Robert Shurtleff. Her new identity worked. But once she was a soldier, she had a new problem: to stay disguised. She treated her own wounds, for example. But eventually, she needed a doctor. Although the doctor reported her, she wasn't punished. Instead, the Massachusetts General Court gave her an honorable discharge and paid her.

5   These bold colonial women were problem-solvers. Adams tried to influence Congress by writing letters to her husband. The women at Valley Forge strengthened the army. Finally, Sampson showed she could fight as a woman. These women helped the women and girls of the future.

Brand X Pictures/Stockbyte/Getty Images

EXPOSITORY ESSAY

Paragraph 4

Underline a source that Keya uses. How does the information from her source support her central idea?

_____

_____

_____

What is an example of a transitional word or phrase she uses to connect her ideas?

_____

_____

Paragraph 5

Reread the conclusion. **Underline** the evidence that reinforces the central idea.

Apply the Rubric

With a partner, use the rubric on page 200 to discuss why Keya scored a 4 on her essay.

My Goal I can write an expository essay.

Analyze the Prompt

Writing Prompt

Write an expository essay to explain to your class about how inventors improved society.

Purpose, Audience, and Task Reread the writing prompt. What is your purpose for writing? My purpose is to _____

_____

Who will your audience be? My audience will be _____

_____

What type of writing is the prompt asking for? _____

_____

Set a Purpose for Reading Sources Asking questions about the ways inventors improved society will help you figure out your purpose for reading. It also helps you understand what you already know about the topic. Before you read the following passage set about inventions, write a question here.

_____

_____

_____

_____

Steve Debenport/E+/Getty Images

Read the following passage set.

BENJAMIN FRANKLIN'S
Bifocals

1   Benjamin Franklin was known for inventing things. A thinker and scientist, he thought of inventions to improve people's health and well-being. One of these inventions is bifocals, or "double spectacles," as he called them. **Bifocals are glasses that help people see near and far clearly.**

2   Franklin invented bifocals because he had vision problems. He needed to wear one pair of glasses to see close up and a different pair to see far away. He was tired of frequently changing his glasses. He came up with an ingenious idea. First, he asked an optician to cut the lenses in half for his two different sets of glasses. He then combined a half lens from each into a single frame. The half lens that allowed him to see near was on the bottom, and the half lens that improved his distance vision was on the top. His idea was practical—and still in use in the twenty-first century today.

Benjamin Franklin's Sketch

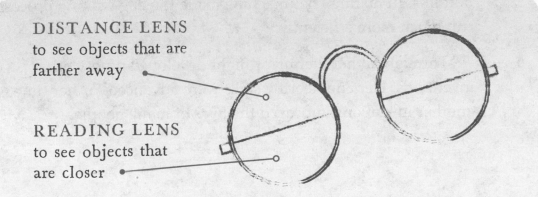

DISTANCE LENS
to see objects that are farther away

READING LENS
to see objects that are closer

Courtesy National Gallery of Art – Washington

FIND TEXT EVIDENCE 🔍

Paragraph 1
Read the highlighted central idea.
Underline the ways that Franklin's invention helped him.

Paragraph 2
Circle the words that signal the steps Franklin took to make the bifocals.
Draw a box around the word that tells you what the author thinks of Franklin's invention.

Benjamin Franklin's Sketch
How does Franklin's sketch help you understand how the bifocals work?

_____

_____

_____

_____

_____

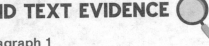 **Take Notes** Paraphrase the central idea of the source, and give examples of supporting details.

WRITING

FIND TEXT EVIDENCE 🔍

Paragraph 3

Underline the central idea. The details that help focus the essay are highlighted.

Paragraph 4

Circle an example of a transitional word or phrase that links two ideas.

Paragraph 5

How did Knight's bag-making machine improve society?

_____

_____

_____

_____

_____

Paragraph 6

Draw a box around the detail that tells you how successful Knight was.

Take Notes Paraphrase the central idea of the source, and give examples of supporting details.

Margaret Knight, ENGINEER AND INVENTOR

3   In 1849, twelve-year-old Margaret Knight was working at a New Hampshire cotton mill when she witnessed a fellow child worker get severely injured by the steel-tipped shuttle of a loom. **She decided to find a way to stop these powerful looms from injuring children. She invented a safety device that prevented injuries at the mill.** Her safety device was the beginning of a long and productive inventing career.

4   Knight had always been fascinated with machines. To create the safety device for the loom, she methodically tested and experimented with different machines. She finally made a device that worked successfully. As a result, it was installed in all of the looms in the mill.

5   Knight didn't stop inventing after she developed the safety device for the loom. In 1867, while working at a paper bag factory, she had another brilliant idea. At the time, paper bags didn't have flat bottoms. They were also made by hand. She designed and built a model of an automatic bag-making machine. Her machine could cut, fold, and glue bags with flat bottoms. In no time, her machine made the bag-making process run much more efficiently.

6   Throughout her lifetime, Knight developed ninety other inventions. Her engineering skills were advanced for her time, and her inventions improved the lives of many people.

HENRY FORD and the MODEL T

7 "I will build a car for the great multitude. It will be large enough for the family, but small enough for the individual to run and take care of. It will be constructed of the best materials, by the best men to be hired, after the simplest designs that modern engineering can devise. But it will be so low in price that no man making a good salary will be unable to own one."

8 Automobile manufacturer Henry Ford famously spoke these words when he introduced his Model T car in 1908. Ford's success in creating a reliable, affordable car transformed the way Americans traveled. Previously, only the wealthy could afford cars. With its improved traction, the Model T was a reliable option, as it could handle rough dirt roads.

9 In 1913, Ford also pioneered new manufacturing processes. The Model T was mass-produced on a moving assembly line. Ford and his team followed basic principles of mass production. One job flowed into the next, so work moved continuously.

10 Ford's processes reduced factory costs. In less than a year, assembly time for each car frame, or structure, dropped from twelve hours to ninety-three minutes. The price of a new Model T dropped, too, from $950 in 1908 to $290 in 1927.

11 For the first time, more Americans, including the working-class, could travel as never before. They had more freedom to travel outside their homes.

FIND TEXT EVIDENCE

Paragraphs 7–8

Underline the central idea. **Draw a box** around the details that support the idea that the Model T transformed travel.

Paragraph 9

What is another way that the Model T changed American society?

_____

_____

_____

Paragraph 10

Circle the fact and detail that provide strong evidence for the central idea.

Paragraph 11

Draw a box around the group that was most affected by the Model T.

Take Notes Paraphrase the central idea of the source and give examples of supporting details.

My Goal I can synthesize information from three sources.

TAKE NOTES

Read the writing prompt below. Use the three sources, your notes, and the graphic organizer to plan a response.

Writing Prompt *Write an expository essay to explain to your class how inventors improved society.*

Synthesize Information

Review the evidence recorded from each source. How does the information show that inventions improved society? Discuss your ideas with a partner.

CHECK IN 1 2 3 4

Plan: Organize Ideas

Central Idea	Supporting Ideas
Inventors designed devices to make people's lives easier and safer.	Inventors designed their devices because they discovered a need for them.

Relevant Evidence

Source 1	Source 2	Source 3
Franklin was frustrated that he had to switch between using two pairs of glasses to see near and far.	Knight witnessed a child getting injured by the steel-tipped shuttle of a loom.	

(bkgd) Valentain Jevee/Shutterstock

Draft: Elaboration

Include Supporting Details Authors use elaboration to develop the central idea. Elaboration may include facts, definitions, examples, or quotations from multiple sources. In the example below from "Creating a Nation," the author gives details about Thomas Jefferson.

> Jefferson knew he had to convince many colonists of the need for independence. As a result, he combined a variety of ideas to make his case. Individuals, he explained, had certain rights. These included life, liberty, and the pursuit of happiness. Governments were created to protect those rights.

Now use the above paragraph as a model to write about the ways inventors improved society. Try to use details to support your central idea in your paragraph.

_____

_____

_____

 Draft Use your graphic organizer and the example above to write your draft in your writer's notebook. Before you start writing, review the rubric on page 200. Remember to indent each paragraph.

Grammar Connections

As you write your draft, use verb tenses correctly when you describe inventors of the past. Remember to use past tense verbs consistently to connect these events that occurred at the same time: *Franklin discovered how to make a lightning rod. He also designed a Franklin stove.*

CHECK IN   1   2   3   4

Revise: Peer Conferences

Review a Draft Listen actively to your partner. Take notes about what you liked and what was difficult to follow. Begin by telling what you liked. Use these sentence starters.

I like the details you used to support the central idea because . . .
What did you mean by . . .
I think adding a fact can support this idea because . . .

After you finish giving each other feedback, reflect on the peer conference. What suggestion did you find to be the most helpful?

_____

_____

_____

Revision Use the Revising Checklist to help you figure out what text you may need to move, elaborate on, or delete. After you finish writing your final draft, use the full rubric on pages 240–243 to score your essay.

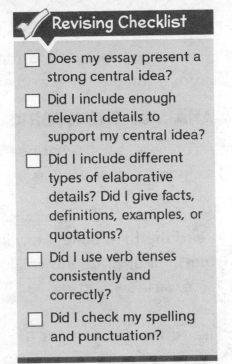

Next, you'll write an expository essay on a new topic.

✓ Revising Checklist

- ☐ Does my essay present a strong central idea?
- ☐ Did I include enough relevant details to support my central idea?
- ☐ Did I include different types of elaborative details? Did I give facts, definitions, examples, or quotations?
- ☐ Did I use verb tenses consistently and correctly?
- ☐ Did I check my spelling and punctuation?

My Score			
Purpose, Focus, & Organization (4 pts)	Evidence & Elaboration (4 pts)	Conventions (2 pts)	Total (10 pts)

WRITE TO SOURCES

You will answer an expository prompt using sources and a rubric.

ANALYZE THE RUBRIC

A rubric tells you what needs to be included in your writing.

Purpose, Focus, and Organization
Read the third bullet. How can transitional strategies link ideas in an expository text?

Transitional strategies _____
_____
_____

Read the third and fourth bullets. What is the connection between using transitions and using a logical text structure to organize ideas?

_____
_____
_____

Evidence and Elaboration
Underline the words that tell you what kind of vocabulary you should include in your expository essay.

Expository Writing Rubric

Purpose, Focus, and Organization • Score 4

- stays focused on the purpose, audience, and task
- clearly presents and fully develops the central idea about a topic
- uses transitional strategies, such as words and phrases, to connect ideas
- uses a logical text structure to organize information
- begins with a strong introduction and ends with a strong conclusion

Evidence and Elaboration • Score 4

- effectively supports the central idea with convincing facts and details
- has strong examples of relevant evidence, or supporting details, from multiple sources
- uses elaborative techniques, such as facts, examples, definitions, and quotations from sources
- expresses interesting ideas clearly using precise language
- **uses appropriate academic and domain-specific language**
- uses different sentence structures

Turn to page 240 for the complete Expository Writing Rubric.

Academic Language

Choose Appropriate Words Academic language is formal language that you can use when writing in subjects such as math or reading. It is frequently used in written expository, argumentative, and literary texts. Strong writers use academic vocabulary to focus the topic of their essays.

Read the paragraph below. Examples of academic language are highlighted in bold text.

> Alexander Hamilton was a Federalist who strongly **supported** ratifying, or adopting, the Constitution. Hamilton, John Jay, and James Madison secretly wrote and published *The Federalist Papers*, **encouraging** their fellow delegates to ratify the Constitution. As a result, *The Federalist Papers* had a direct **impact** on the delegates. The Anti-Federalists immediately **responded** by proclaiming the Constitution would have too much power over the states' **individual** rights. The Federalists then **addressed** their opponents' objections and **defended** the strength of a national government, finally winning the vote for ratification.

Read the paragraph above. What do these words tell you about the focus of this paragraph?

_____

_____

_____

Audience

When strong writers draft a piece of work, they make choices about their vocabulary and language based on their audience. For example, if you are describing a process, you might use the phrase *set up* with your friends, but you might use the academic word *establish* with a teacher. Reread the paragraph about Hamilton. Who do you think the audience is? How do these words convey a more precise meaning?

WRITING

ANALYZE THE STUDENT MODEL

Paragraph 1

Read the first paragraph of Marc's essay. Examples of academic language are highlighted. Reread these words. What do they tell you about the topic of Marc's essay?

_____

_____

_____

Paragraph 2

Underline a specific fact from a source. What is an example of relevant evidence, or supporting detail, that Marc uses to support his central idea?

_____

_____

_____

Paragraph 3

Circle the detail that tells you how Ma's team is trying to achieve their goal.

Student Model: Expository Essay

Marc responded to the Writing Prompt: _Write an expository essay to present to your class about what people do to accomplish difficult goals._ Read Marc's essay below.

1   Saving the planet. **Achieving** world peace. Finding a **solution** to a physics **experiment**. These three **goals** seem almost impossible to **accomplish**. But **research** shows that breaking a goal into smaller chunks will help people to succeed.

2   According to the article "Motivation in the Middle," researchers found that people do well at the beginning and end of a task. A graph in the article shows a sharp dip when people get to the middle of a task. Then the lines on the graph go up again as they finish it. The middle is the problem. So what's the solution? Researchers suggest breaking goals or projects into smaller daily chunks. This way people feel productive when they meet the smaller goal, and eventually they will achieve their larger goal. I'm going to try this method the next time I have a big science project due!

3   Tammy Ma is a physicist. She was interviewed about her team's goal to harness fusion energy into ignition. Achieving this goal could be a way to produce clean electricity and heat. Ma's team breaks down this goal by setting up experiments and then analyzing the data. However, they often make mistakes. But Ma says, "We always learn from our mistakes or previous findings. You have to keep asking 'why?' and find ways to test a hypothesis to get to a final answer."

4   Ma says this testing is "fun." She also says that when they test new designs, they learn something they didn't understand before.

5   According to the article "The Goal of Peace," athletes also break down big goals into smaller tasks. Both Tegla Loroupe and Martin Strel are world-class athletes who wanted to make the world a better place. Loroupe is an Olympian marathoner from Kenya. Since 2003, her organization has been sponsoring peace marathons. She used her experience in training and goal setting to help promote peace among warring tribes in Kenya, Uganda, and Sudan. Strel is a champion swimmer who swims in polluted rivers to raise awareness about water pollution. Both took the sport that they loved and used it to achieve a bigger goal.

6   People can achieve what seem like impossible goals. The trick is to break your big project into smaller chunks. Each time you finish a small goal, you are closer to your bigger goal. However, like Ma said, you should always learn from your mistakes!

AVAVA/Shutterstock

Paragraphs 3–4

Underline a technique of elaboration that Marc uses. What is an example of academic language?

_____

_____

_____

Paragraph 5

What is an example of a transitional word or phrase that Marc uses to connect his ideas?

_____

_____

Paragraph 6

Reread the conclusion. **Underline** the phrase that Marc repeats from paragraph 1.

Apply the Rubric

With a partner, use the rubric on page 212 to discuss why Marc scored a 4 on his essay.

Analyze the Prompt

Writing Prompt

Write an expository essay to print in your school newspaper about the ways humans protect the environment.

Purpose, Audience, and Task Reread the writing prompt. What is your purpose for writing? My purpose is to _____

_____

Who will your audience be? My audience will be _____

_____

What type of writing is the prompt asking for? _____

_____

Set a Purpose for Reading Sources Asking questions about the different ways humans protect the environment will help you figure out your purpose for reading. It also helps you understand what you already know about the topic. Before you read the passage set about the ways humans care for nature and wildlife, write a question here.

_____

_____

_____

Read the following passage set.

GOING Above and Beyond

1   Most of us **experience** our planet from our homes, neighborhoods, and schools. But two men have gone above and beyond, literally, to teach us more about Earth.

2   Brian Duffy is an astronaut and space shuttle pilot who has flown four missions with NASA. One of his missions helped scientists **understand** more about the sun's **effect** on Earth's atmosphere. Spending forty days total in space changed Duffy's **point of view** about Earth, humans, and nature. From space, he could see how small our planet really is. He could see how our thin atmosphere protects our fragile planet. He could even see the Amazon rain forest being cleared and burned from 220 miles above. "With each flight I went on, there was less and less green, and there was always smoke burning it off," Duffy said.

3   Marty Snyderman is a photographer and diver. He goes into the depths of the oceans to photograph sharks and whales. His photographs raise awareness about their vital role in the marine ecosystem. Overfishing caused the decline of many shark populations around the world. Since these animals cannot speak for themselves, Snyderman decided to become their "voice" through his photography. He says, "I wanted the world to know, and more importantly to act."

4   Whether we are in the air, on land, or in the water, Duffy said it best when he remarked, "We are all in this together, so we all have a responsibility to look after our home planet."

Catmando/Shutterstock

EXPOSITORY ESSAY

FIND TEXT EVIDENCE

Paragraphs 1–2
Read the highlighted academic language in paragraphs 1 and 2.

Paragraph 2
Circle what Duffy sees from space that is being burned. Why is it important that Duffy points out this fact?

_____

_____

_____

Paragraphs 3–4
How does Duffy's perspective compare to Snyderman's?

_____

_____

_____

_____

Take Notes Paraphrase the central idea of the source and give examples of supporting details.

Paragraph 5

Draw a box around the detail that tells what unusual ointment the Loggerhead Marinelife Center gives to wounded turtles.

Paragraph 6

Reread this paragraph. Examples of academic language are highlighted. What do these words tell you about the focus of this passage?

_____

_____

Paragraph 7

Circle the signal words or phrase that links the ideas in paragraphs 6 and 7.

Paragraph 8

Underline the details that tell how the center protects the environment.

📝 **Take Notes** Paraphrase the central idea of the source, and give examples of supporting details.

THE TURTLE LADY OF Juno Beach

5   When people think of honey, they usually think of a sweet snack, but for a facility in Florida that treats wounded sea turtles, honey is used as a medicine! The Loggerhead Marinelife Center rescues and rehabilitates sea turtles. When the turtles are healthy, they are released back to the sea. Sometimes they leave with honey in their wounds, which bonds well with water and helps them heal.

6   The center was **founded** by "the Turtle Lady" Eleanor Fletcher. Fletcher and her husband worked in real estate in Juno Beach. Sea turtles nested on the shore below their office. Fletcher saw hatchlings move toward land instead of toward the sea. She **researched** and learned that the turtles were walking toward land because of the bright lights that people had built along the beaches. The lights confused the hatchlings, so Fletcher put a stop to them. Then she started **educating** children and adults about turtle conservation and protection.

7   At first, she did a lot of the work herself. She opened her home to visitors, giving tours and showing marine specimens. She taught herself how to categorize and count turtle nests. She even confronted poachers and chased them away.

8   Eventually, she founded the Loggerhead Marinelife Center. The center welcomes school field trips, outreach programs, and summer camps. Over 300,000 guests come each year to view the exhibits and visit the turtle hospital. The facility has an outdoor classroom, research labs, a resource center, a park, and a store. The exhibits and programs highlight South Florida's wildlife and marine environments.

COMMUNITY BIRD SCIENTIST

SOURCE 3

9   In 1896, Harriet Hemenway and Minna Hall founded the Massachusetts Audubon Society to help protect waterbirds from future harm. Their efforts helped shape the national Audubon Society, which continues to protect birds and their habitats.

10   One of the society's programs is the Great Backyard Bird Count (GBBC). The GBBC is a global event over a weekend in February. It is run by the society and the Cornell Lab of Ornithology. First, participants register on the GBBC website. These "community scientists" are then asked to go bird-watching in their backyards for fifteen minutes or more during that weekend. Bird-watchers use field guides and bird-watching apps to identify each bird species they've seen. People all over the world complete checklists. They record their local bird sightings on the GBBC eBird database. Ornithologists still use this data to help with bird conservation.

Top 5 State Bird Count Listings

State	Number of Species	Number of Checklists
California	373	8,530
Texas	361	6,785
New York	171	6,520
Pennsylvania	145	5,953
Florida	290	5,612

Data totals as of March 14, 2018.

Feng Yu/iStock/Getty Images

EXPOSITORY ESSAY

FIND TEXT EVIDENCE 🔍

Paragraph 9
Underline the detail that tells why Hemenway and Hall founded the Audubon Society.

Paragraph 10
Circle the signal words that list the steps in the order in which participants complete checklists.

Top 5 State Bird Count Listings
What do you notice about the number of species and the number of checklists when you compare the findings across these five states?

_____

_____

_____

_____

_____

📝 **Take Notes** Paraphrase the central idea of the source, and give examples of supporting details.

My Goal I can synthesize information from three sources.

TAKE NOTES

Read the writing prompt below. Use the three sources, your notes, and the graphic organizer to plan a response.

Writing Prompt *Write an expository essay to print in your school newspaper about the ways humans protect the environment.*

Synthesize Information

Review the evidence recorded from each source. How does the information show that humans protect the environment? Discuss your ideas with a partner.

CHECK IN 1 2 3 4

Plan: Organize Ideas

Central Idea	Supporting Ideas
People protect the environment through conservation and awareness.	People founded organizations to teach others about the importance of ecosystems.

Relevant Evidence

Source 1	Source 2	Source 3
Astronaut Brian Duffy saw that humans were affecting the environment. Photographer Marty Snyderman took pictures of sharks to show people that sharks are part of vital marine ecosystems.	Eleanor Fletcher founded the Loggerhead Marinelife Center. She taught children and others about turtle conservation and marine environments.	

Draft: Transitions

Connect Ideas Transitional strategies such as signal words and phrases help to connect ideas in an essay. Organizational structures are used to connect ideas, too. For example, in a cause-and-effect text structure, the cause tells why something happens, and the effect tells what happens.

Signal words and phrases like *because, so, since, due to,* and *as a result* will help to describe cause-and-effect relationships.

Read the sentences below.

> We collected water samples from the river. We wore gloves to collect the samples. Because toxic chemicals from the mill had flowed into the river by accident, we didn't want to risk catching any contaminants.

Read the third sentence above. The transitional word *because* is used to connect the two ideas. Rewrite the first two sentences into one sentence. Use a transitional word or phrase to connect the two ideas.

_____

_____

_____

Draft Use your graphic organizer and the example above to write your draft in your writer's notebook. Before you start writing, review the rubric on page 212. Remember to indent each paragraph.

Grammar Connections

Do not confuse prepositions with transitional words or phrases. Prepositions include *in, over, about, under,* and *on.* Prepositional phrases begin with a preposition, end with a noun or pronoun, and can function as an adjective or an adverb: *The plant <u>with four leaves</u> is toxic. We study the plant <u>in the forest.</u>*

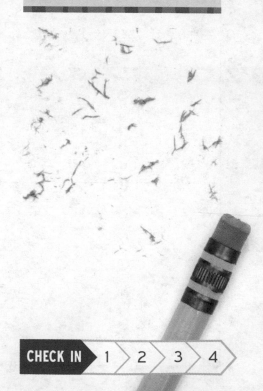

CHECK IN ⟩ 1 ⟩ 2 ⟩ 3 ⟩ 4

Revise: Peer Conferences

Review a Draft Listen actively to your partner. Take notes about what you liked and what was difficult to follow. Begin by telling what you liked. Use these sentence starters.

I like the evidence you used to support the central idea because . . .
What did you mean by . . .
I think adding transitions help to . . .

After you finish giving each other feedback, reflect on the peer conference. What suggestion did you find to be the most helpful?

_____

_____

_____

Revision Use the Revising Checklist to help you figure out what text you may need to move, elaborate on, or delete. After you finish writing your final draft, use the full rubric on pages 240–243 to score your essay.

✔ **Revising Checklist**

☐ Did I include academic language?

☐ Did I support my central idea with relevant evidence?

☐ Did I structure my ideas in an organizational order, or pattern?

☐ Did I use transitions to connect ideas? Did I use transitions and prepositions correctly?

☐ Did I check my spelling and punctuation?

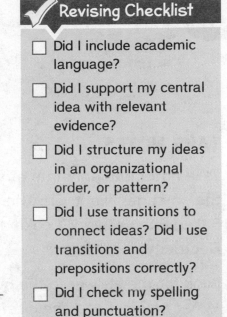

Turn to page 199. Fill in the bars to show what you learned.

My Score			
Purpose, Focus, & Organization (4 pts)	Evidence & Elaboration (4 pts)	Conventions (2 pts)	Total (10 pts)

TAKE NOTES

Take notes and annotate as you read the passages "Popover!: The Ultimate Baked Bubble" and "Cooking with Electricity."

Look for the answer to the question: *What physical and chemical changes in matter might not happen if chefs do not follow instructions for baking and cooking food?*

_____

_____

_____

_____

_____

_____

_____

_____

PASSAGE 1

EXPOSITORY TEXT

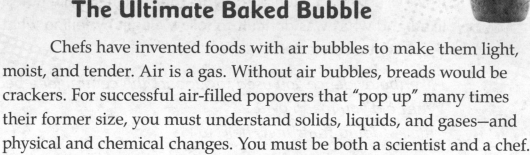

POPOVER!
The Ultimate Baked Bubble

Chefs have invented foods with air bubbles to make them light, moist, and tender. Air is a gas. Without air bubbles, breads would be crackers. For successful air-filled popovers that "pop up" many times their former size, you must understand solids, liquids, and gases—and physical and chemical changes. You must be both a scientist and a chef.

Popovers are made from a batter of flour, milk, eggs, and butter. The flour is a solid. The milk and eggs are liquids. If the butter is solid, melt it. Heating the butter causes a physical change as it turns from a solid into a liquid. Mixing the ingredients is also a physical change.

When you pour the batter into the tins, it is a thin and runny liquid. The heat inside a very hot oven bakes the top first, and then the sides and the bottom of the batter in each tin. It turns the outside batter into a solid while the inside is still liquid. As the batter heats up, it gives off steam, a gas, that can't escape through the well-sealed top crust. The rising steam raises the top crust.

Halfway through baking, turn the temperature down to medium. By this time, the outside of the popover is completely baked, while the inside is still very moist. The moderate heat helps to solidify the inside without burning the outside.

Baking causes a chemical change to the ingredients. The baked dough is a different type of matter than the ingredients. By studying the properties of solids, liquids, and gases, chefs use temperature changes and physical and chemical changes to bake popovers!

COOKING with Electricity

Chefs use different tools to create delicious treats like popovers. Many of the tools and appliances in a kitchen use electricity. The wires are plugged into the kitchen's electrical circuit. Turning on a switch closes the circuit, allowing electricity to flow through the circuit and power the device.

TAKE NOTES

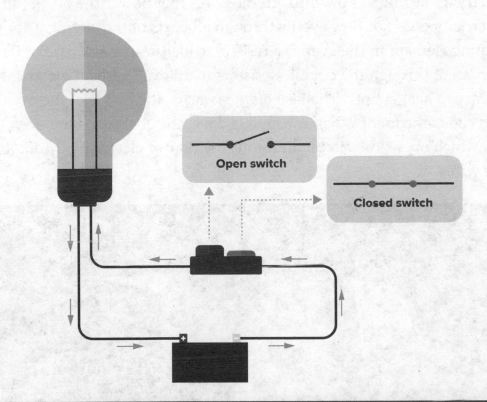

Open switch

Closed switch

A circuit must be closed for electrical devices such as light bulbs to work. The arrows in the diagram show the direction in which electrons flow through the circuit. The current is considered to flow in the opposite direction.

NWM/Shutterstock

TAKE NOTES

_____

_____

_____

_____

_____

_____

_____

_____

_____

_____

_____

_____

_____

_____

_____

_____

_____

The wires that power these devices are made of a type of material called a conductor. A conductor is a material that allows electric charges to move easily through it. Copper is a metal that is a good conductor. Copper wires are commonly used in appliances and covered with plastic. The plastic is an insulator, which does not conduct electricity. This keeps the wire safe so that the electric current only flows through the wire and prevents a dangerous short circuit, which could start a fire.

When a chef turns on an electric oven, the circuit is closed, and electricity begins to flow through the wires that power the oven. But electricity does not flow evenly through all parts of the circuit. The heating element in the oven is a resistor, which works against the flow of current through the circuit. Resistors in an oven convert electrical energy to heat energy. The heat energy warms the inside of the oven and cooks the food! When the food is done, the chef turns the oven off, which opens the circuit and stops the flow of electricity through the wires.

(b) kickstand/E+/Getty Images; (inset) kickstand/E+/Getty Images

COMPARE THE PASSAGES

Review your notes from "Popover!: The Ultimate Baked Bubble" and "Cooking with Electricity." Use your notes and the Venn diagram below to record how the information in both texts is alike and different.

Alike

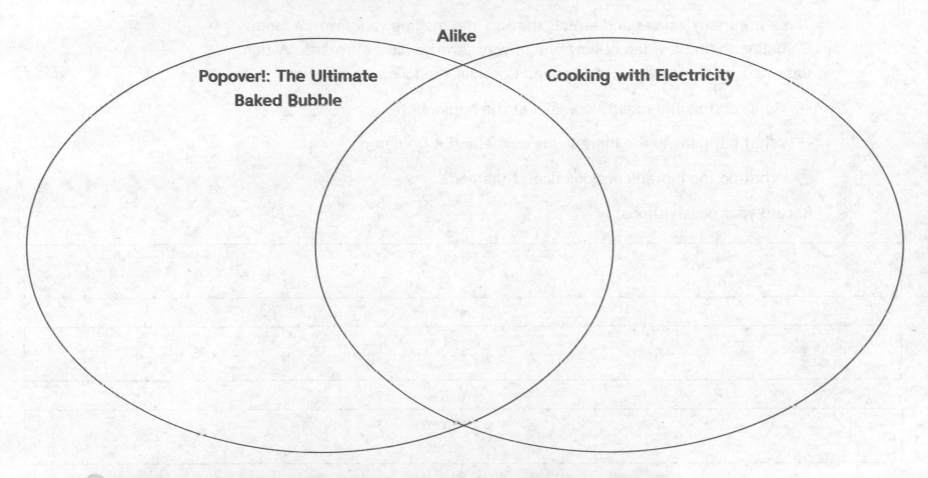

Popover!: The Ultimate Baked Bubble

Cooking with Electricity

Synthesize Information

Think about both texts. What information in both texts helps you understand how chefs use scientific principles in the kitchen? Write your response in your reader's notebook.

CHECK IN ▸ 1 ⟩ 2 ⟩ 3 ⟩ 4 ⟩

MAKE OBSERVATIONS

Scientists make observations about the world around them. They observe changes that occur and then investigate to understand what causes those changes.

There are many causes and effects that go into making your favorite foods. Go online to find a video of how one of your favorite dishes is made. Watch the video, and observe what happens. Consider the following questions:

- What do the ingredients look like at the beginning?

- What happens to the ingredients as the dish is prepared?

- What do the ingredients look like at the end?

Record your observations.

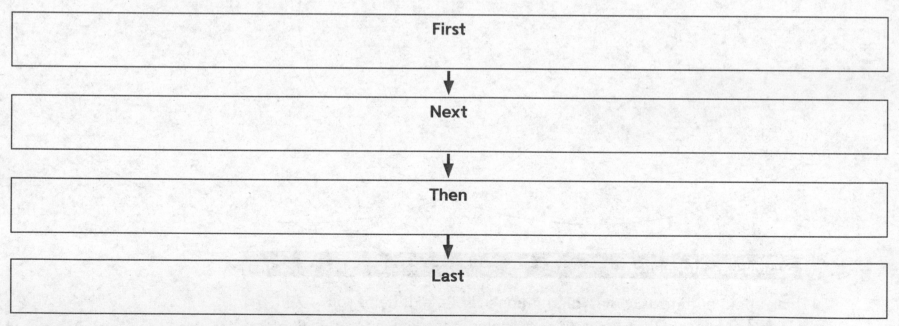

First

↓

Next

↓

Then

↓

Last

After you have observed all the steps in preparing your recipe, discuss with your partner how the ingredients changed. Why did they change?

EXPLAIN YOUR OBSERVATIONS

What causes and effects did you observe while your dish was prepared?
Describe your observations in the circles and boxes below.

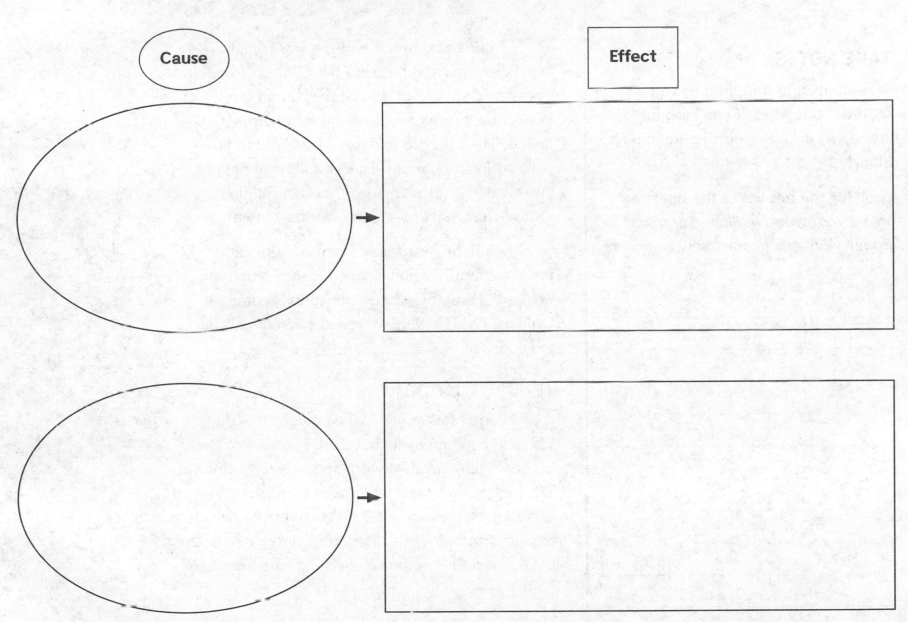

Cause

Effect

My Goal I can read and understand social studies texts.

TAKE NOTES

Take notes and annotate as you read the passages "Searching for Freedom" and "Supporting Religious Liberty."

Look for the answer to the question: *What motivated William Penn and Roger Williams to start new colonies?*

_____

_____

_____

_____

_____

_____

_____

_____

_____

_____

PASSAGE 1

INFORMATIONAL TEXT

Searching for FREEDOM

In England in the 1600s, it was illegal to belong to any church except the Church of England. Those who spoke out against the church faced persecution, or harsh treatment for their religious beliefs. The Pilgrims and the Puritans both faced persecution, and many decided to leave England and head to North America. Another religious group—the Quakers—also faced persecution.

William Penn came from a wealthy and powerful family who belonged to the Church of England. Penn, however, decided to become a Quaker. The Quakers were very tolerant of other religions.

A Debt Repaid

Penn's father had loaned money to King Charles II. When his father died, Penn asked the king to repay this debt with land in North America. The king gave him a large piece of land located west of New Jersey. Penn called it Pennsylvania, which means "Penn's Woods." He founded a colony where Quakers—and everyone else—could worship freely.

FREE LIBRARY OF PHILADELPHIA/Alamy Stock Photo

Peace and Diversity

Unlike many other European settlers, Penn dealt fairly with Native Americans. He signed a peace treaty with the Lenni-Lenape tribe and paid them for their lands. Penn welcomed Native American refugees from other colonies, too. Because of Penn, the colony was peaceful for a long time.

From its earliest days, Pennsylvania welcomed ethnic and religious diversity. The name Penn chose for the first capital of Pennsylvania reflects his Quaker beliefs. He called it Philadelphia, which means "city of brotherly love."

PASSAGE **2**

INFORMATIONAL TEXT

Supporting Religious LIBERTY

In the early 1630s, a minister in the Puritan colony of Massachusetts held discussions about freedom of religion. The minister, named Roger Williams, also criticized the colony's close bond between church and government.

Williams's criticism made the Puritan government officials angry. They threatened to arrest him and ship him back to England if he did not stop. He promised not to speak publicly, but he continued to speak freely at home. In 1635, the officials decided that Williams had violated his promise. They banished him from the colony, and Williams was forced to leave Massachusetts—and

TAKE NOTES

CONNECT TO CONTENT

TAKE NOTES

_____

_____

_____

_____

_____

_____

_____

_____

_____

_____

_____

_____

_____

_____

_____

_____

_____

_____

his family.

Williams then traveled south of Boston and bought land from the Narragansett Native Americans. In 1636, he established a colony in what is now Rhode Island.

In 1644, Williams's colony took the revolutionary step of granting liberty to all of its inhabitants, including Jews, Native Americans, and other non-Christians. The colonial charter promised that no person would be "punished, disquieted, or called in question for any differences in opinion on matters of religion."

Rhode Island was also the first American colony to guarantee separation of church and state. Williams's colony remained a sanctuary for people of all faiths throughout the colonial era.

Roger Williams was forced to leave his family when he was banished from the colony of Massachusetts in 1635.

COMPARE THE PASSAGES

Review your notes from "Searching for Freedom" and "Supporting Religious Liberty." Create a Venn diagram like the one below. Use your notes and the diagram to record how the information in both texts is alike and different.

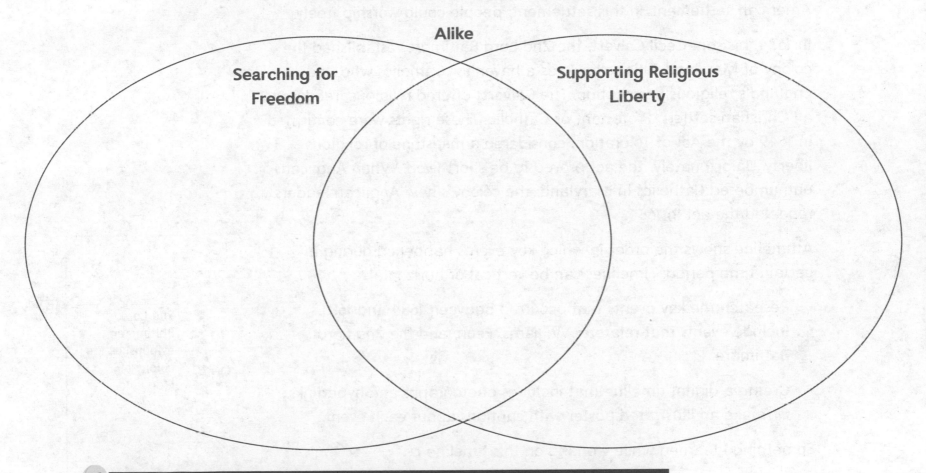

Alike

Searching for
Freedom

Supporting Religious
Liberty

Synthesize Information

Think about both texts and what you read earlier about the foundation of the U.S. How were Penn's and Williams's problems similar to those of the writers of the Constitution? Write a reply in your reader's notebook.

CHECK IN 1 2 3 4

MAKE A TIMELINE

Williams's and Penn's colonies weren't the only ones that offered religious choice. In 1632, the Catholic-practicing George Calvert, the 1st Lord Baltimore, was granted a charter by England's King Charles I for a North American settlement. In this settlement, people could worship freely.

In 1634, his son, Cecil Calvert, the 2nd Lord Baltimore, established the colony of Maryland. This colony was a haven for Catholics who fled England's religious persecution. The Calverts offered religious freedom to all Christian settlers, Protestant or Catholic. These rights were confirmed in 1649 by the Act of Toleration, considered a milestone of religious liberty. Unfortunately, the act proved to be short-lived. When Anglicans outnumbered Catholics in Maryland, the colony's new Anglican leaders repealed the act in 1654.

A timeline shows the order in which key events happened during a certain time period. Timelines can be vertical or horizontal.

- Research the key events that occurred between 1634 and 1681. Include events that relate to Williams, Penn, and the 2nd Lord Baltimore.

- Create a digital timeline that includes photographs and hyperlinks. Or make an illustrated poster with captions about each event.

Something I learned while working on this timeline is

_____

_____

_____

_____

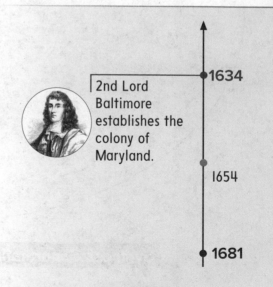

2nd Lord Baltimore establishes the colony of Maryland.

1634

1654

1681

DigitalVision Vectors/Getty Images

Reflect on Your Learning

Talk About It Reflect on what you learned in this unit. Then talk with a partner about how you did.

I am really proud of how I can _____

_____

_____

_____

Something I need to work more on is _____

_____

_____

_____

_____

My Goal Set a goal for Unit 3. In your reader's notebook, write about what you can do to get there.

Share a goal you have with a partner.

Argumentative Writing Rubric

Score	Purpose, Focus, and Organization (4-point Rubric)	Evidence and Elaboration (4-point Rubric)	Conventions of Standard English (2-point Rubric begins at score point 2)
4	• stays focused on the purpose, audience, and task • makes a claim that clearly supports a perspective • uses transitional strategies, such as words and phrases, to connect ideas • presents ideas in a logical progression, or order • begins with a strong introduction and ends with a strong conclusion	• effectively supports the claim with logical reasons • has strong examples of relevant evidence, or supporting details, from multiple sources • uses elaborative techniques, such as examples, definitions, and quotations from sources • expresses interesting ideas clearly using precise language • uses appropriate academic and domain-specific language • uses different sentence structures	

Score	Purpose, Focus, and Organization (4-point Rubric)	Evidence and Elaboration (4-point Rubric)	Conventions of Standard English (2-point Rubric begins at score point 2)
3	• generally stays focused on the purpose, audience, and task • makes a claim that mostly supports a perspective • uses some transitional strategies, such as words and phrases, to connect ideas • presents ideas in a mostly logical progression, or order • begins with an acceptable introduction and ends with a sufficient conclusion	• mostly supports the claim with some logical reasons • has some examples of mostly relevant evidence, or supporting details, from multiple sources • uses some elaborative techniques, such as examples, definitions, and quotations from sources • generally expresses interesting ideas using both precise and general language • mostly uses appropriate academic and domain-specific language • mostly uses different sentence structures	

Argumentative Writing Rubric

Score	Purpose, Focus, and Organization (4-point Rubric)	Evidence and Elaboration (4-point Rubric)	Conventions of Standard English (2-point Rubric)
2	• stays somewhat focused on the purpose, audience, and task, but may include unimportant details • does not make a clear claim or does not completely support a perspective • uses few transitional strategies to connect ideas • may present ideas that do not follow a logical progression, or order • may begin with an inadequate introduction or end with an unsatisfactory conclusion	• shows some support of the claim with logical reasons • has weak and inappropriate examples of evidence or does not include enough sources • may not use elaborative techniques effectively • expresses some interesting ideas, but ideas are simple and vague • uses limited academic and domain-specific language • may use only simple sentence structures	• has a sufficient command of grammar and usage • has a sufficient command of capitalization, punctuation, spelling, and sentence formation • has slight errors in grammar and usage that do not affect meaning

(bkgd) Valentain Jevee/Shutterstock

Score	Purpose, Focus, and Organization (4-point Rubric)	Evidence and Elaboration (4-point Rubric)	Conventions of Standard English (2-point Rubric)
1	• is not aware of the purpose, audience, and task • does not make a claim or does not support a perspective • uses few or no transitional strategies to connect ideas • does not present ideas in a logical progression, or order • does not include an introduction nor a conclusion	• supports the claim with few logical reasons or does not support the claim at all • has few or no examples of evidence or does not include enough sources • does not use elaborative techniques • has confusing or unclear ideas or does not express any interesting ideas • does not demonstrate a grasp of academic and domain-specific language • consists only of simple sentence structures	• has an incomplete command of grammar and usage • has an incomplete command of capitalization, punctuation, spelling, and sentence formation • has some errors in grammar and usage that may affect meaning
0			• does not have a command of grammar and usage • does not have a command of capitalization, punctuation, spelling, and sentence formation • has too many serious errors in grammar and usage that frequently disrupt meaning

Expository Writing Rubric

Score	Purpose, Focus, and Organization (4-point Rubric)	Evidence and Elaboration (4-point Rubric)	Conventions of Standard English (2-point Rubric begins at score point 2)
4	• stays focused on the purpose, audience, and task • clearly presents and fully develops the central idea about a topic • uses transitional strategies, such as words and phrases, to connect ideas • uses a logical text structure to organize information • begins with a strong introduction and ends with a strong conclusion	• effectively supports the central idea with convincing facts and details • has strong examples of relevant evidence, or supporting details, from multiple sources • uses elaborative techniques, such as facts, examples, definitions, and quotations from sources • expresses interesting ideas clearly using precise language • uses appropriate academic and domain-specific language • uses different sentence structures	

Score	Purpose, Focus, and Organization (4-point Rubric)	Evidence and Elaboration (4-point Rubric)	Conventions of Standard English (2-point Rubric begins at score point 2)
3	• generally stays focused on the purpose, audience, and task • presents and develops the central idea about a topic in a mostly clear and complete way, although there may be some unimportant details • uses some transitional strategies, such as words and phrases, to connect ideas • uses a mostly logical text structure to organize information • begins with an acceptable introduction and ends with a sufficient conclusion	• mostly supports the central idea with some convincing facts and details • has some examples of mostly relevant evidence, or supporting details, from multiple sources • uses some elaborative techniques, such as facts, examples, definitions, and quotations from sources • generally expresses interesting ideas using both precise and general language • mostly uses appropriate academic and domain-specific language • mostly uses different sentence structures	

Expository Writing Rubric

Score	Purpose, Focus, and Organization (4-point Rubric)	Evidence and Elaboration (4-point Rubric)	Conventions of Standard English (2-point Rubric)
2	• stays somewhat focused on the purpose, audience, and task, but may include unimportant details • does not clearly present or develop a central idea • uses few transitional strategies to connect ideas • may not follow a logical text structure to organize information • may begin with an inadequate introduction or end with an unsatisfactory conclusion	• shows some support of the central idea with few convincing facts and details • has weak and inappropriate examples of evidence or does not include enough sources • may not use elaborative techniques effectively • expresses some interesting ideas, but ideas are simple and vague • uses limited academic and domain-specific language • may use only simple sentence structures	• has a sufficient command of grammar and usage • has a sufficient command of capitalization, punctuation, spelling, and sentence formation • has slight errors in grammar and usage that do not affect meaning

Score	Purpose, Focus, and Organization (4-point Rubric)	Evidence and Elaboration (4-point Rubric)	Conventions of Standard English (2-point Rubric)
1	• is not aware of the purpose, audience, and task • does not have a central idea • uses few or no transitional strategies to connect ideas • does not follow a logical text structure to organize information • does not include an introduction nor a conclusion	• supports the central idea with few facts and details or does not support the central idea at all • has few or no examples of evidence or does not include enough sources • does not use elaborative techniques • has confusing or unclear ideas or does not express any interesting ideas • does not demonstrate a grasp of academic and domain-specific language • consists only of simple sentence structures	• has an incomplete command of grammar and usage • has an incomplete command of capitalization, punctuation, spelling, and sentence formation • has some errors in grammar and usage that may affect meaning
0			• does not have a command of grammar and usage • does not have a command of capitalization, punctuation, spelling, and sentence formation • has too many serious errors in grammar and usage that frequently disrupt meaning